S0-ARN-684

Be My Disciples

Peter M. Esposito
President

Jo Rotunno, MA
Publisher

Anne P. Battes, M.Ed.
Associate Publisher

Program Advisors
Michael P. Horan, PhD
Elizabeth Nagel, SSD

GRADE ONE
SCHOOL EDITION

"The Subcommittee on the Catechism, United States Conference of Catholic Bishops, has found this catechetical series, copyright 2014, to be in conformity with the *Catechism of the Catholic Church*."

NIHIL OBSTAT
Rev. Msgr. Robert Coerver
Censor Librorum

IMPRIMATUR
† Most Reverend Kevin J. Farrell DD
Bishop of Dallas
March 5, 2013

† IN MEMORIAM

Dedicated to James Bitney, 1947–2013, creative, contributing writer and editor for Grades 1 and 2 of the *Be My Disciples* series as well as many other RCL Benziger curriculum series over the years.

The *Nihil Obstat* and *Imprimatur* are official declarations that the material reviewed is free of doctrinal or moral error. No implication is contained therein that those granting the *Nihil Obstat* and *Imprimatur* agree with the contents, opinions, or statements expressed.

Acknowledgments

Excerpts are taken and adapted from the *New American Bible* with Revised New Testament and Revised Psalms ©1991, 1986, 1970, Confraternity of Christian Doctrine, Washington, D.C., and are used by permission. All rights reserved. No part of the *New American Bible* may be reproduced in any form without permission in writing from the copyright owner.

Excerpts are taken or adapted from the English translation of the *Rite of Baptism*, ©1969; *Rite of Confirmation* (Second Edition), ©1975, International Commission on English in the Liturgy, Inc. (ICEL). All rights reserved.

Excerpts are taken and adapted from the English translation of the *Roman Missal*, ©2010, International Commission on English in the Liturgy, Inc. (ICEL) All rights reserved.

Excerpts and adaptations of prayers were taken from the book of *Catholic Household Blessings & Prayers*, © 2007, United States Conference of Catholic Bishops, Washington, D.C. All rights reserved. No part of the book of *Catholic Household Blessings & Prayers* may be reproduced or transmitted in any form or by any means, electronic or mechanical, including photocopying, recording, or by any information storage and retrieval system, without permission in writing from the copyright holder.

Copyright © 2014 RCL Publishing LLC

All rights reserved. *Be My Disciples* is a trademark of RCL Publishing LLC. This publication, or parts thereof, may not be reproduced in any form by photographic, electronic, mechanical, or any other method, for any use, including information storage and retrieval, without written permission from the publisher. Send all inquiries to RCL Benziger, 8805 Governor's Hill Drive, Suite 400, Cincinnati, OH 45249.

Toll Free   877-275-4725
Fax   800-688-8356

Visit us at www.RCLBenziger.com
BeMyDisciples.com

20761 ISBN 978-0-7829-1634-8 (Student Edition)
20771 ISBN 978-0-7829-1640-9 (Teacher Edition)

2nd Printing.
May 2014.

Contents

Welcome to
Be My
✝Disciples!

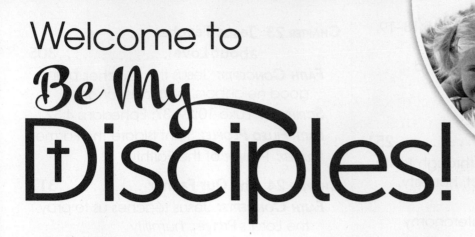

Jesus wants you to be his **disciple!** He wants you to know about him and follow him. This year you will learn many new things about Jesus. You will learn how to be a good disciple.

All About Me
My name is

_____

- -

_____.

I am a child of God.

Unit 1: We Believe, Part One
You will learn about God's Son, Jesus.
Look on page 52. Find out the name of Jesus' mother.
Trace her name on the line.

_____

- - - - - - - - - - Mary -

_____

Unit 2: We Believe, Part Two
We will learn about the Holy Trinity.
Look on page 94. Find out the name of the helper Jesus promised to send. Trace the helper's name on the line.

_____

Holy Spirit

Unit 3: We Worship, Part One

You will learn that each of the Church's seasons tell us something about Jesus.

Look on page 125. Find out when the Church celebrates that Jesus was raised from the dead. Trace the word on the line.

Easter

Unit 4: We Worship, Part Two

You will learn how our Church celebrates and prays. Look on page 200. Learn the name of the most important celebration of the Church. Trace the word on the line.

Mass

Unit 5: We Live, Part One

You will learn how to live the Ten Commandments. Look on page 246. Learn which Commandment teaches us to worship only God. Trace the word on the line.

First

Unit 6: We Live, Part Two

You will learn to live as a child of God.

Look on page 322. Learn who gave us the Our Father. Trace the name on the line.

Jesus

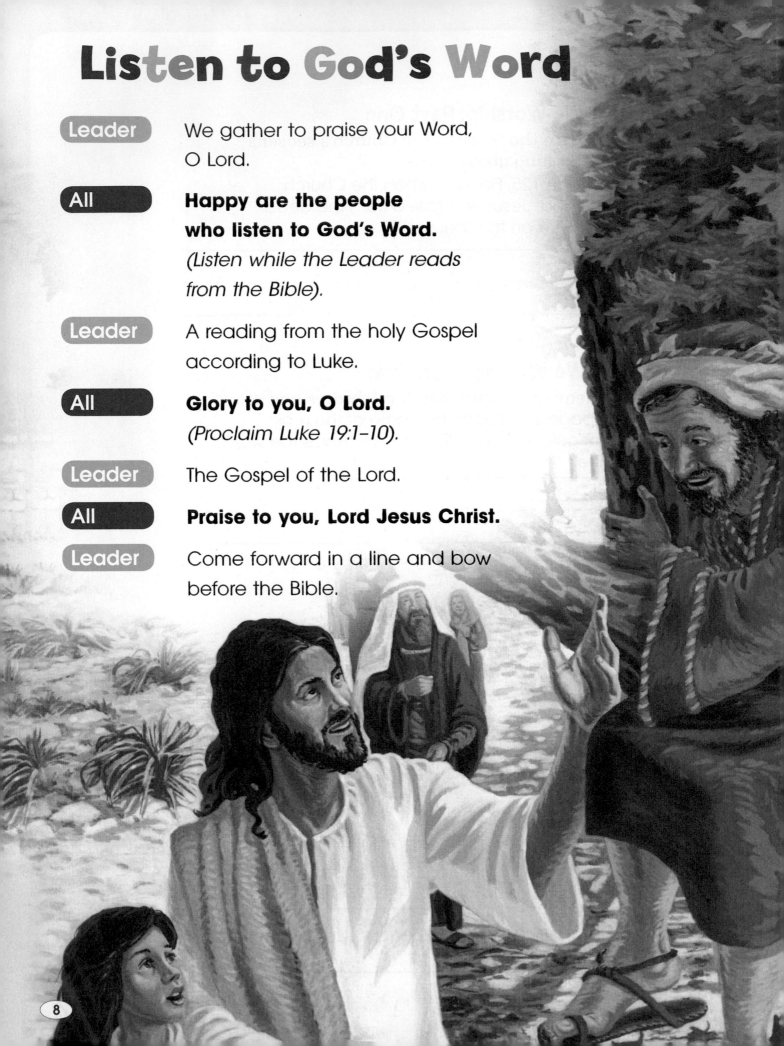

Listen to God's Word

Leader   We gather to praise your Word, O Lord.

All   **Happy are the people who listen to God's Word.** *(Listen while the Leader reads from the Bible).*

Leader   A reading from the holy Gospel according to Luke.

All   **Glory to you, O Lord.** *(Proclaim Luke 19:1–10).*

Leader   The Gospel of the Lord.

All   **Praise to you, Lord Jesus Christ.**

Leader   Come forward in a line and bow before the Bible.

Time for Children

The day was getting late. Jesus was tired. His friends wanted him to rest. But moms and dads started bringing their children to see Jesus. Jesus' friends said to them, "Go away. Jesus is tired. He has no time for children now."

"Wait!" Jesus said to his friends. "I always have time for children. Let the children come to me."

The children rushed to Jesus. Jesus welcomed and blessed them all. Jesus said with a big smile, "Look, this is what heaven is like."

BASED ON MARK 10:13–16

What I Know

What is something you already know about these faith words?

Creation

_____

- -

_____

Jesus

_____

- -

_____

Put an X next to the faith words you know.
Put a ? next to the faith words you need to learn more about.

____ Bible   ____ kindness   ____ Creator

____ faith   ____ Son of God   ____ wonder

A Question I Have

What question would you like to ask about the Bible?

_____

- -

_____

- -

_____

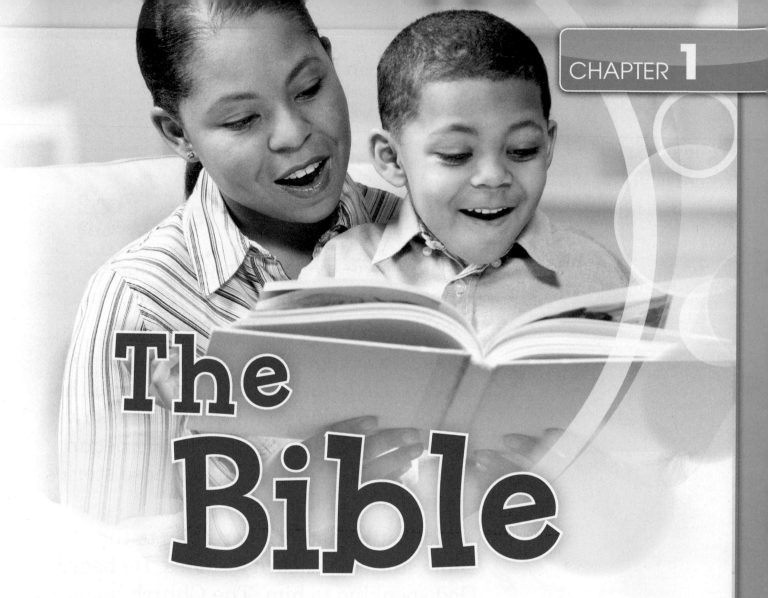

CHAPTER 1

The Bible

? What is a favorite book that someone reads to you? Why is it your favorite?

When we listen to a story from the Bible, we hear God's Word to us. In the Bible we read:

Listen to God's word and keep it. Then you will be blessed.

BASED ON LUKE 11:28

? What do these words from the Bible ask you to do?

Disciple Power

Faithful

Good friends of Jesus are faithful to him. They are loyal to him. They listen to him. They do what he said and did.

Saint Augustine

Augustine lived many years ago. When he was young, he often got into trouble. He made many bad choices.

One day, Augustine was sitting in his garden. He heard a child's voice sing the words, "Take and read!" Augustine saw his mother's Bible on a table. He began to read it. He thought about these stories and began to follow Jesus.

Augustine listened carefully to the Bible stories he heard at Mass. He heard God speaking to him. The Church honors him today as Saint Augustine.

? What happened when Augustine read the Bible?

Activity

The Bible Teaches

Decorate the Bible.
Write your name on the lines below.
Then read the sentence.

HOLY BIBLE

HOLY BIBLE

The Bible teaches

_____

- - - - - - - - - - - - - - - - - - -

_____

how to be a good and
faithful friend of Jesus.

About the Bible

We have many books. But the **Bible** is the most special book.

God chose people to help write the Bible. The Bible is the written Word of God. It is a holy book because it is God's very own Word to us. The Bible also tells us about God's love for us.

The Bible tells us many things about God. The Bible tells something important about God. Listen to these words from the Bible.

God is love.
God showed his love to us.
God sent us Jesus his Son.
Jesus told us to love one another.

BASED ON 1 JOHN 4:8–9, 21

❓ Why is the Bible such a special book?

Learning About God

At Mass, we listen to readings from the Bible. The priest or deacon helps us understand what we heard. This helps us learn about God.

 What are some ways we can learn about God?

Catholics Believe

Readings at Mass

God speaks to us through the Bible. The readings at Mass teach us about God's love and help us learn how to follow Jesus.

Activity Draw or write about your favorite story from the Bible. Share your story with a partner.

A Man Learns about God

One day a man was reading the Bible. Philip was a follower, or disciple, of Jesus. He saw the man and ran up to him.

Philip asked, "Do you understand what you are reading?"
The man said, "No. I need help."
Philip told the man about God's love.
Philip told the man about Jesus.
The man became a follower of Jesus.
He became a member of the Church.

BASED ON ACTS OF THE APOSTLES 8:26–40

? What did Philip tell the man?

A Follower of Jesus

Philip helped the man understand a story in the Bible. He helped the man become a follower of Jesus.

The Bible helps us learn about God. Our parents, teachers, priests, and deacons help us understand what we hear in the Bible. This helps us learn how to follow Jesus.

? Who helps you to follow Jesus?

Faith-Filled People

Saint Philip the Apostle

Philip was one of the first twelve Apostles. The Apostles were the first leaders of the Church. Philip was a curious man. He wanted to know everything he could about Jesus and his teachings.

Activity

When the Bible is read to you, what do you do? Trace the dotted lines to find out.

listen

Followers of Jesus Show Love

Jesus told his followers about God's love. Jesus showed God's love by caring for them. Jesus asked his followers to love one another. Jesus said:

> "As I have loved you, so you also should love one another. This is how all will know that you are my disciples."
>
> JOHN 13:34b–35

❓ What are the ways you follow Jesus?

Activity Put a check (✔) by the pictures of the children showing love for one another. They are listening to Jesus' words in the Bible.

The Bible is God's Word to you. When you listen to the Bible at Mass, God is speaking to you. When you and your family read the Bible at home, God is speaking to you. When you do these things, you are a faithful and loyal follower of Jesus.

I Follow Jesus

Activity

Reading God's Word

Draw you and your family reading the Bible at home.

My Faith Choice

Check (√) how you will listen to God speaking to you in the Bible.

This week, I will

☐ listen to the readings at Mass.

☐ ask someone to read a Bible story to me.

Pray, "Thank you, Holy Spirit, for helping me listen to the Word of God and follow Jesus. Amen."

TO HELP YOU REMEMBER

1. The Bible is God's Word to us.

2. Stories in the Bible teach us about God's love.

3. We listen to the Bible at Mass.

Recall

Draw lines to finish the sentences.

1. The Bible tells us about   Word of God.

2. We hear the Word of God   God's love for us.

3. The Bible is the written   follow Jesus.

4. Augustine read the Bible and began to   at Mass.

Reflect

What will people see you do as you live as a follower of Jesus this week?

_____

_____

_____

_____

_____

_____

_____

Share   **Share one way that you can read the Bible more often with your family.**

A Listening Prayer

Leader   O God, open our ears.
Help us listen to your Word.

All   **Help us listen to your Word.**

Leader   O God, open our eyes.
Help us to see your love in the world.

All   **Help us to see your love in the world.**

Leader   O God, open our minds.
Help us to learn more about you.

All   **Help us to learn more about you.**

Leader   Listen to the Word of God.
Then think about what you hear.

Reader   *Children, obey your parents [in the Lord], for this is right. "Honor your father and mother."*

EPHESIANS 6:1–2a

Reader   The word of the Lord.

All   **Thanks be to God.**

21

With My Family

This Week . . .

In Chapter 1, "The Bible," your child learned:

▶ God is the real author of the Bible.

▶ The Bible is the inspired, written Word of God.

▶ The Holy Spirit inspired the human writers of the Bible to assure that God's Word would be accurately communicated.

▶ The faithful follower of Jesus reads the Bible and follows the teachings of the Church.

For more about related teachings of the Church, see the *Catechism of the Catholic Church*, 101–133, and the *United States Catholic Catechism for Adults*, pages 11–15.

■ Sharing God's Word

Read together Acts of the Apostles 8:26–40 about Philip the Apostle. Or read the adaptation of the story on page 16. Talk about why it is important to read the Bible every day.

■ We Live as Disciples

The Christian home and family is a school of discipleship. Choose one or both of the following activities to do as a family, or design a similar activity of your own.

▶ Throughout the week choose a time to read the Bible as a family. Talk about ways the Bible passage or story you read helps your family live as a Catholic family.

▶ Help your child develop good habits that help him or her become a faithful follower of Jesus. Build on the things your child is already doing, for example, praying each day, helping out at home with chores, or treating others kindly.

■ Our Spiritual Journey

In this section, you will learn some of the major spiritual disciplines of the Church. These disciplines help us form the good habits of living as faithful followers of Jesus. Daily prayer is one of those disciplines. In this chapter, your child prayed and listened to Scripture. Read and pray together the prayer on page 21. This type of prayer is called *lectio divina*.

For more ideas on ways your family can live as disciples of Jesus, visit **BeMyDisciples.com**

CHAPTER 2

God Loves Us

? Name the people who know and love you. How do they show you that they love you?

The Bible tells us that God loves us. Listen to these words from the Bible about God's love for you.

Lord, you see me and know me.
You know when I sit and when I stand.
You know what I think and where I go.
You know everything I do.

BASED ON PSALM 139:1–6

? What do these words say about God?

Generosity

Followers of Jesus are generous. We share our things with others. We pray for them. We are generous to them.

The Church Follows Jesus

Saint Rose of Lima

Read to Me

Rose knew and loved God. She knew that God loved her. She helped others know about God's love.

Rose lived with her family in Lima in the country of Peru. Rose helped take care of the family garden. She grew flowers and food. She sold flowers and gave the money to the poor and the sick. This made them feel better.

Rose was kind and generous. She helped people learn how much God loved them.

? How did Saint Rose show others that God loved them?

Sharing God's Love

Saint Rose of Lima showed us how to love God and help others. You can pray to Saint Rose. Ask her to help you share God's love.

Activity
You can show God's love. In each of the three flowers, draw or write one way you can be generous to others.

Faith Focus
Who helps us to know God and believe in him?

Faith Words

faith
Faith is a gift from God. It helps us to know God and to believe in him.

believe
To believe means to have faith in God. It means to give yourself to God with all your heart.

We Know God Loves Us

God knows us and loves us all the time. God wants us to know and love him too.

The Bible has many stories of people who had **faith** in God. They listened to God. They came to know and **believe** in him. They loved him with all their hearts.

Here is a Bible story about faith. Abraham and Sarah lived a long time before Jesus. God chose Abraham to be a great leader. God made him a promise. God said,

You will be the father of many nations. I will bless you and your wife Sarah. You will soon become the parents of a son.

BASED ON GENESIS 17:4, 15–16

What did God promise Abraham?

Faith in God

Abraham and Sarah listened to God and did what he asked. They had faith in God and believed in his promises.

? What is one way that we show our faith in God?

Isaac

Isaac is the son whom God promised Abraham and Sarah. The name Isaac means "he laughs." Isaac brought much joy and happiness to his parents.

Activity

Sharing Faith

Abraham and Sarah told everyone about God's love. Draw the people who share their faith and tell you about God's love.

Jesus Helps Us to Know God

Many years after Abraham and Sarah died, God sent his Son Jesus to us. Jesus is the Son of God.

Jesus helps us best to know God and his love. Jesus helps us to believe in God and have faith in him.

Jesus taught over and over how much God loves us. He taught us that God is love. Jesus said,

"Whoever loves me will keep my word, and my Father will love him."

JOHN 14:23

? What did Jesus teach us about God?

Our Family Helps Us to Know God

God knows and loves every person. God wants everyone to know him and love him, too.

God gave us the gift of a family. Our family helps us to grow in our faith. They help us to know God and believe in him.

Our family helps us give ourselves to God with all our hearts. Our family helps us to grow in faith.

Catholics Believe

Sign of the Cross

Catholics pray the Sign of the Cross. This shows we have faith in God. We pray, "In the name of the Father, and of the Son, and of the Holy Spirit. Amen."

Activity

Trace the words. Discover one important thing about God.

God
loves us.

Faith Focus
Who helps us to know
and love God?

Faith Words
▶ **pray**
We pray when we
listen and talk to God.

Our Church Helps Us to Know God

We belong to the Catholic Church. Our parish is our Church family. Our parish is our home in the Catholic Church. People in our Church know and love God. They help us to know and love him too.

We **pray** together. We listen to the Bible. We learn about Jesus and God's love. We help each other.

❓ How does your Church help you come to know God?

Your family and the Church help you to learn how much God loves you. You can help your family and friends learn how much God loves them. You can treat them the way Jesus asked. You can be kind and generous to them.

Activity

Sharing God's Love

In one heart, draw people helping you learn about God. In the second heart draw yourself sharing God's love.

My Faith Choice

Check (✓) what you will do. This week I will help others know how much God loves them. I will

☐ tell others about God.

☐ show my family I love them.

☐ thank God for his love.

 Pray, "Thank you, Holy Spirit, for helping me to show my love for God. Amen."

1. God's gift of faith helps us come to know him and believe in him.

2. Jesus is the Son of God. He helps us to know how much God loves us and to have faith in God.

3. Our family and our Church help us to know, love, and serve God.

Chapter Review

Recall

Complete the sentences. Color the ☐ *next to the best choice.*

1. To _____ means to have faith in God.

   ☐ believe   ☐ hope

2. _____ is the Son of God.

   ☐ Abraham   ☐ Jesus

3. Faith is a gift from _____.

   ☐ our friends   ☐ God

4. _____ helps us best to know God and his love.

   ☐ Jesus   ☐ The Bible

Reflect

What are the ways that God shows his love for you?

_____

- -

_____

_____

- -

_____

Share | Tell a partner one way you will share your love for God and your family.

Sign of the Cross

We pray the Sign of the Cross to begin our prayers.
Pray the Sign of the Cross with your class.

In the name of the Father,

and of the Son,

and of the Holy Spirit.

Amen.

Leader

O God, we call you Father.
You are the God of Love.

O God, we call you Jesus,
the Son sent from above.

O God we call you Spirit,
You help us all to know

That we are all your children,
And that you love us so.

All

In the name of the Father,
and of the Son,
and of the Holy Spirit.
Amen.

With My Family

This Week . . .

In Chapter 2, "God Loves Us," your child learned:

▶ God has revealed himself and invites us to believe in him and his love for us.

▶ Jesus Christ revealed the most about God and his love for us.

▶ Jesus is the Son of God. He is the fullness of God's Revelation.

▶ Our family and our Church help us grow in faith in God and in love for him.

For more about related teachings of the Church, see the *Catechism of the Catholic Church*, 80–95 and 142–175, and the *United States Catholic Catechism for Adults*, pages 35–47.

Sharing God's Word

Read together John 13:34–35 from your family Bible or from a children's version of the Bible. Emphasize that when we treat one another as Jesus told his disciples to do, we show our love for God and for one another. We also show others how much God loves them.

We Live as Disciples

The Christian home and family is a school of discipleship. It is the first place where children learn to live as disciples. Choose one or more of the following activities to do as a family, or design a similar activity of your own.

▶ Compile a list of the names of people who have helped or who are helping your family grow in faith and in your love for God. Pray for these people at a family meal.

▶ Name the ways your family is generous to each other and to other people. Remind your children that when they are generous they are living as Jesus taught.

Our Spiritual Journey

Generosity is a habit of being a disciple of Christ. Generously sharing our spiritual and material blessings with others, especially people in need, is one of the foundational spiritual disciplines, or practices, of the Christian life. This discipline is known as almsgiving. Make this discipline one of the hallmarks of your family's life. Pray together: Dear Jesus, give us generous hearts. Amen.

For more ideas on ways your family can live as disciples of Jesus, visit **BeMyDisciples.com**

CHAPTER 3

God, Our Father and Creator

? What is your favorite part of creation?

Close your eyes and see all the beautiful things in the world. Listen to what the Bible tells us about the world.

O God, everything you made is wonderful!

BASED ON PSALM 136:4

? What do these words from the Bible tell you about the world God made?

Disciple Power

Wonder

The word "wonderful" comes from the word "wonder." Wonder is a special gift from God. God gives us this gift to help us come to know how good he is.

Kateri Tekakwitha

Kateri was born in the state of New York. When Kateri was four years old, her eyes were harmed by an illness. She could hardly see in the sunlight.

The people of her village gave Kateri the nickname Tekakwitha. The name means "The one who walks trying to find her way."

Kateri loved the outdoors. She helped grow corn, beans, and squash. She picked roots of plants in the forest to make medicines. The beauty of the forest reminded her of God. It filled her with wonder. Kateri went there to talk with God and listen to him.

The Catholic Church honors her as Saint Kateri Tekakwitha. The things she did and said show us how to live as disciples of Jesus.

❓ Why was being in the forest important to Kateri?

Activity

Wonderful Gifts

Some wonderful things are hidden in this forest.
Each is a gift from our wonderful loving God.
Find and circle each gift: a moon, a bird, a flower, a
bee, a fish, and a horse. Then color the picture.

Faith Words
Creator
God is the Creator. He made everything out of love and without any help.

God Creates a Wonderful World

God made the ☀ for warmth and light. God made the 🌙 and ⭐ to shine at night.

God made the 🌍 and then planted 🌳, while up in the sky flew the 🕊 and the 🐝.

God grew the 🌸 up from the earth. Sweet 🍇 and 🍎 came to birth.

God made the 🐟 in the waters to swim.

God made the 🐒 out on the limb. Soon 🦁 and 🐯 and 🐻 did appear, then 🐐 and 🐔, and 🐑, and 🦌.

God made them all. No one else could.

God made them and loved them and called them all good.

BASED ON GENESIS 1:1–25

❓ What did God do with all of creation?

38

God the Creator

God made our wonderful world. God is the **Creator**. God alone made Heaven and Earth. He made everything out of love. The Bible tells us,

God looked at everything he had made, and he found it very good.

GENESIS 1:31

Remember, God is love. God the Creator is also our loving Father. God shares his love with us now and forever.

Catholics Believe

The Our Father

The Church prays the Our Father every day. We pray the Our Father at Mass. We tell God we love him. We tell God we know he loves and cares for us.

Activity Think of your favorite part of God's creation. Draw a picture of it. Share what it tells you about God.

Faith Focus
Why did God create
people?

Faith Words
▶ **image of God**
We are created in the
image of God. We
are children of God.

God Creates People

God is the Creator of all people. He creates every person to be an **image of God.** In the Bible we read,

God made people in his image. He blessed them and told them to take care of everything he made. God said everything he made was very good.

BASED ON GENESIS 1:26–31

God loves every person. We are very special to God. He created us to be happy with him now on Earth and forever in Heaven.

❓ Why are you special to God?

40

Activity

I Am Special

Draw yourself in the flower.
Write your name on the line.
Then pray your prayer.

Dear God,

You know my name.

_____

- -

_____

I am so special to you.
Thank you, God.
Amen.

Faith-Filled People

Saint Catherine of Siena

Catherine enjoyed the wonders of creation. Things in nature reminded Catherine how much God loves us. This helped her to grow in her love for God. The Church celebrates the feast day of Saint Catherine of Siena on April 29.

41

God Is Our Loving Father

Every person is created by God. God the Creator is our loving Father.

This is why the Bible tells us we are children of God.

Jesus helped us to know and believe that God is our Father. He taught us to pray, "Our Father, who art in heaven . . ."

BASED ON MATTHEW 6:9

God the Father loves us and knows each of us by name. Jesus told us that God the Father cares for all his creation. He cares for people.

We show we love God our Father when we take care of ourselves. We show our love for God when we take care of creation.

❓ How do we show our love for God?

God Loves Me.
I Love God.

God is wonderful. He is so very good to us. The world is God's gift to everybody. One way you can say thank you to God is to help take care of the things in the world.

Activity

Caring for God's Creation

In the puzzle piece draw a picture of yourself taking care of something in God's creation.

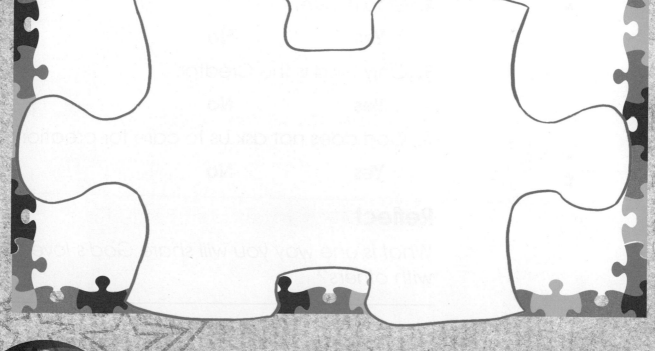

My Faith Choice

This week, I will take care of God's creation. I will try to do what I have drawn in the puzzle.

Pray, "Thank you, God. Thank you for the gift of your creation. Amen."

1. God is the Creator. He made the whole world out of love.

2. God created people in the image of God.

3. Jesus taught us that God is our Father.

Chapter Review

Recall

Draw lines to complete the sentences.

1. Jesus   made everything out of love.

2. People   taught us to call God our Father.

3. God

          are made in the image of God.

*Circle **Yes** if the sentence is true.*
*Circle **No** if it is not true.*

4. God is love.

   Yes   **No**

5. Only God is the Creator.

   Yes   **No**

6. God does not ask us to care for creation.

   Yes   **No**

Reflect

What is one way you will share God's love with others?

_____

- -

_____

_____

- -

_____

Share — **Tell your teacher how you will treat others with kindness this week.**

Thank You, God!

A rebus prayer uses pictures to help us pray.
Use a word for each picture. Pray the prayer together.

All　　　**Thank you, God, for your ❤.**

Reader 1　You made the ☀.

All　　　**Thank you, God, for your ❤.**

Reader 2　You made the 🌙 and the shining ⭐.

ALL　　　**Thank you, God, for your ❤.**

Reader 3　You made the ⛰ and 🌳.

All　　　**Thank you, God, for your ❤.**

Reader 4　You made the 🐟 and 🐅.

All　　　**Thank you, God, for your ❤.**

Reader 5　You made all the world's 👨‍👩‍👧‍👦.

All　　　**Thank you, God, for your ❤.**
　　　　　　You made ME!

BASED ON PSALM 148

With My Family

This Week . . .

In Chapter 3, "God, Our Father and Creator," your child learned:

▶ God is the Creator. All God's creation is good. Everything good exists because God created it out of love.

▶ God created every person in his image. He created people with all their differences.

▶ God is our Father. There is no limit to his love for his children.

▶ We respond to God the Creator's love by helping to take care of creation.

For more about related teachings of the Church, see the *Catechism of the Catholic Church*, 232–248 and 268–314, and the *United States Catholic Catechism for Adults*, pages 53–56, 67–68.

Sharing God's Word

Read together the Bible story in Genesis 1:26–31 about the creation of people. Or read the adaptation of the story on page 38. Emphasize that every person is an image of God.

We Live as Disciples

The Christian home and family is a school of discipleship. It is the first place where children learn to live as disciples. Choose one or more of the following activities to do as a family, or design a similar activity of your own.

▶ God created each person out of love. Take turns sharing what you like about each person.

▶ Invite your child to take part in keeping your home clean. Explain how this is one way of thanking God for his many gifts to your family.

Our Spiritual Journey

Prayer is one of the main spiritual disciplines of the Christian life. Giving thanks to God is one of the five main forms of prayer. Invite everyone to close their eyes and see their favorite part of creation. Then think of how much God loves them, and silently pray, "God, you are so wonderful."

For more ideas on ways your family can live as disciples of Jesus, visit **BeMyDisciples.com**

CHAPTER 4

Jesus, the Son of God

? How do you celebrate your birthday?

Birthdays are wonderful days. Saint Luke tells us about the birthday of Jesus. Mary and Joseph came to Bethlehem. They had to sleep in a stable with the animals. During the night Jesus was born.

> [Mary] wrapped him in swaddling clothes and laid him in a manger, because there was no room for them in the inn.
>
> LUKE 2:7

? What else do you know about the birth of Jesus?

Kindness

We live the virtue of kindness by treating others as we want to be treated.

The Church Follows **Jesus**

We Have Room! Read to Me

Daniella and everyone in San Carlos were excited. It was almost time for Christmas. It was time to celebrate Las Posadas.

For nine nights, the people walked together in the streets. Two people were chosen to be Mary and Joseph. Everyone walked behind them. They carried lighted candles.

Mary and Joseph knocked on many doors. Joseph said, "My wife will soon have a baby. Do you have room for us in your home?" All answered, "We have no room." Finally, one family said to Joseph, "We have room! Come in."

Daniella was more excited. Her family was was the one who answered, "We have room! Come in."

? How did Daniella and her family show kindness to Mary and Joseph?

Activity

Welcome Jesus!

Help Mary and Joseph go from door to door. Help them find room at the house of Daniella and her family. Find letters along the way. Write them in order on the lines below. They will help you send a message of kindness to Jesus.

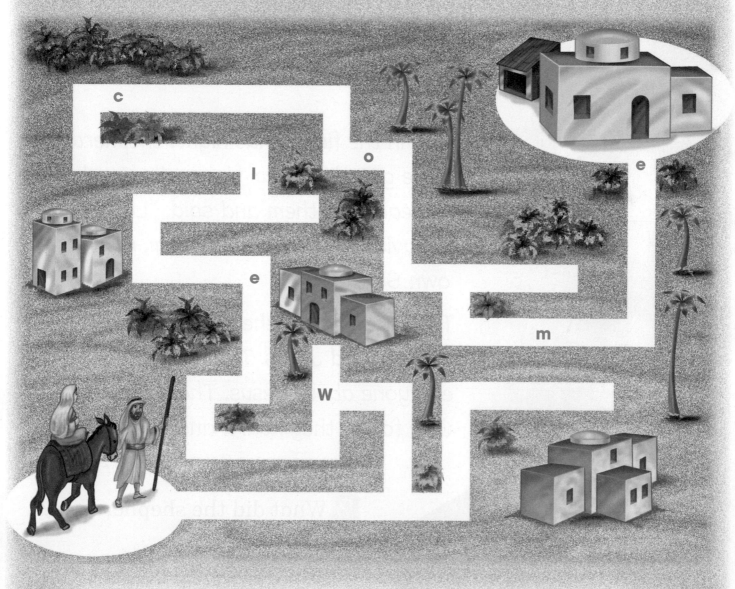

_____

- -

_____ Jesus!

Faith Words
Son of God
Jesus is the Son of God. Jesus is truly God and truly man.

The Son of God

At Christmas each year we remember and celebrate the birth of Jesus. Jesus is the only son of Mary and the **Son of God**. Jesus is truly God and truly man.

The Bible tells us that angels told shepherds about the birth of Jesus. We read,

Out in the fields that night, shepherds were guarding their sheep. An angel appeared to them and said, "Listen! A savior is born in Bethlehem, God's own Son."

The shepherds rushed and found Mary, Joseph, and Jesus. Then they told everyone about Jesus. They praised God for all they heard and saw.

BASED ON LUKE 2:8–17, 20

? **What did the shepherds do?**

Share the Good News!

The shepherds treated Mary, Joseph, and Jesus with kindness. They told others about the birth of Jesus. Then the shepherds shared God's love with people.

We share God's love when we treat others with kindness. One way we can share God's love is at Mass when we pray.

? **What are the ways that you share God's love?**

Catholics Believe

Lord, Have Mercy

At Mass we pray, "Lord, have mercy." Mercy is another word for kindness. Jesus told us that people who are kind and show mercy are blessed by God.

Activity

Draw a picture of yourself telling others about Jesus. Do what the shepherds did.

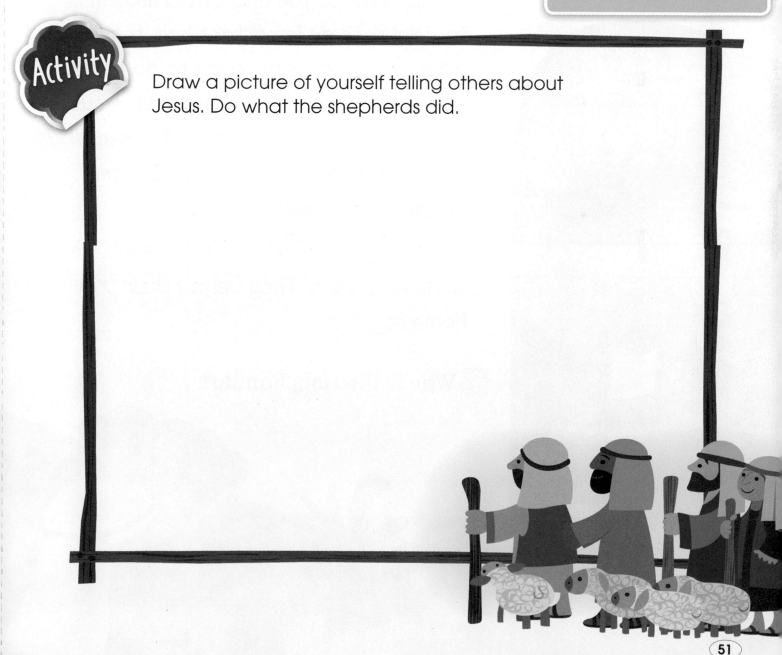

The Holy Family

Mary is the Mother of Jesus, the Son of God. Joseph is the foster father of Jesus. We call Jesus, Mary, and Joseph the **Holy Family**. The Holy Family lived in a town called Nazareth.

Here is a story from the Bible about Jesus as a young boy.

Jesus was twelve years old. The Holy Family went to the city of Jerusalem to celebrate an important holy feast. When everyone was ready to go home, Mary and Joseph could not find Jesus. They finally found him in the Temple. He was listening to the teachers and asking them questions.

When Jesus saw Mary and Joseph, he went with them. They began their trip home together.

BASED ON LUKE 2:41–52

? Who is the Holy Family?

Sharing Love

Mary and Joseph showed their love for Jesus. They took very good care of Jesus as he was growing up. Jesus grew in his love of God and of people.

 **What are the ways that your parents and family show their love for you?**

Faith-Filled People

Saint Anne and Saint Joachim

Anne and Joachim were the parents of Mary. They were the grandparents of Jesus. They helped Mary to love and trust God. The Church celebrates the feast day of Saint Anne and Saint Joachim on July 26.

Activity

Write the names *Jesus, Mary,* and *Joseph* under their pictures.

_____ _____ _____

- - - - - - - - - - - - - - - - - - - - - - - -

_____ _____ _____

Jesus Shares God's Love

When Jesus grew up, he taught others about God. He shared God's love with everyone.

Jesus showed us how to treat people. Jesus treated everyone with kindness and respect. Respect means to treat every person as a child of God.

We are to treat everyone with kindness and respect. We are to share God's love with people.

? Why should we treat every person with kindness and respect?

Activity

Color the ♡s next to the pictures of people showing kindness and respect.

God is always kind to people. Jesus shared God's kindness with people. You are a disciple of Jesus. You are kind to people. You treat them with respect. When you do these things, you are a sign of God's love.

I Follow Jesus

Activity

In the kite draw yourself being kind to someone.

I Am Kind

My Faith Choice

This week, I will do what I drew in the kite. I will

_____

- -

_____

Pray, "Thank you, Holy Spirit, for helping me to be kind to others as Jesus taught. Amen."

1. Jesus is the only son of Mary and the Son of God.

2. The family of Jesus, Mary, and Joseph is the Holy Family.

3. Jesus shared God's love with everyone.

Chapter Review

Recall

Circle the word that best completes each sentence.

1. Jesus is the _____ of God.

     Son   **angel**

2. _____ is the Mother of Jesus.

     Anne   **Mary**

3. _____ is the foster father of Jesus.

     Joachim   **Joseph**

Draw lines to complete the sentences.

4. Jesus is   Jesus, Mary, and Joseph.

5. The Holy Family is   truly God and truly man.

6. We are to treat others with   kindness.

Reflect

How will you treat others this week?

_____

- -

_____

_____

- -

_____

Share   **Talk with a classmate about two ways you can be kind and welcome others.**

Jesus, I Love You

We show that we love Jesus by treating people as he did. Pray this prayer together as a class.

Leader   Let us pray together that our families find ways to help each other. Let us share Jesus' love and tell him that we love him too.

All   **Families help each other.
Families share their fun.
We work and pray together.
Jesus makes us one.**

Leader   Let us learn to sign this prayer:

Jesus

"Jesus, I love you."

Pray the prayer in the morning and at night. Teach your family to sign the prayer. Ask them to pray it with you.

I love you.

With My Family

This Week . . .

In Chapter 4, "Jesus, the Son of God," your child learned:

▶ Jesus is the only son of Mary and the Son of God.

▶ Gabriel announced to Mary that she would become the mother of the Savior, the Son of God, who she was to name Jesus.

▶ The Son of God became truly human without giving up being God. This mystery of faith is called the Incarnation. Jesus is truly God and truly man.

▶ We call Jesus, Mary, and Joseph the Holy Family. Jesus' life in the Holy Family prepared him for the work the Father sent him to do.

For more about related teachings of the Church, see the *Catechism of the Catholic Church*, 456–478 and 512–560, and the *United States Catholic Catechism for Adults*, pages 77–87, 143–149.

■ Sharing God's Word

Read together Luke 2:8–20 about the shepherds who rushed to see the newly born Jesus. Or read the adaptation of the story on page 50. Emphasize that Jesus is truly God and truly man. He is the only son of Mary and the Son of God.

■ We Live as Disciples

The Christian home and family is a school of discipleship. It is the first place children learn to be disciples. Choose one or more of the following activities to do as a family, or design a similar activity of your own.

▶ Talk together about the ways that family members are kind to each other. Explain how acts and words of kindness show a person's love for God.

▶ Choose to do a family activity that shows kindness to people who are not members of your family. For example, as a family visit someone who is lonely or help an elderly neighbor.

■ Our Spiritual Journey

The Great Commandment is the guiding precept of the Christian life. It is the summary or foundational principle of human as well as Christian living. In this chapter your child signed an act of love using American Sign Language. Encourage your child to teach you to sign the prayer on page 57.

For more ideas on ways your family can live as disciples of Jesus, visit **BeMyDisciples.com**

The Big Clean-up

Read to Me

WE CARE FOR GOD'S CREATION

God has given us a special job. God wants us to take care of the wonderful gift of his creation. We are to help keep the world beautiful.

One morning the first-grade teacher at Santa Sophia School asked her students, "How can we make our room beautiful?"

The children looked around the room. They saw paper and pencils, crayons and markers scattered on the tables and desks. Books and worksheets, art supplies and flash cards crammed the shelves. The classroom was a mess.

The children said, "We need to clean up our room!" They also decided to brighten up the room with signs of nature. The class set to work.

As they were cleaning, the students and teachers made a plan to recycle too. They used separate trash cans for paper and plastic. That way some of the trash could be reused. Now the classroom looks beautiful and they are caring for God's creation.

59

Making Connections

God wants us to keep the world beautiful. One place we can start is in our classroom. We can bring God's creation inside.

with MATH AND SCIENCE

Plant seeds in potting soil. Use milk cartons cut in half. Find a place in your classroom where the plants will have plenty of light. Measure the plants each day. Keep a chart of the plants' growth. Watch how the plants add beauty to your classroom.

with LANGUAGE ARTS

Use a chart to write down the steps for taking care of the plants. Keep a classroom diary. Take turns writing down sentences to tell how the plants are growing. Describe what they look like.

with CREATIVE ARTS

Act out how plants make God's world a more beautiful place. Show how to take care of plants. Share what happens to the plant if it does not have enough water and sunlight. Show what happens when you take good care of the plants and God's creation.

Faith Action

God wants me to take care of his creation. I can help keep God's world beautiful. I will

_____

- -

_____

Unit 1 Review

A. Choose the Best Word

Complete the sentences. Color the circle next to the best choice

1. The Bible is _____ own Word to us.

○ the Church's   ○ God's

2. Faith is a gift from God that helps us to know

God and to _____ in him.

○ love   ○ believe

3. Jesus treated _____ people with respect.

○ all   ○ some

4. Jesus is the _____ of God.

○ man   ○ Son

5. _____ is the Mother of Jesus.

○ Mary   ○ Anne

B. Show What You Know

Circle the numbers next to the words that tell about Jesus.

1. Son of God

2. Holy Spirit

3. Loving Father

4. taught others about God

5. shared God's love with everyone

C. Connect with Scripture

What was your favorite story about Jesus in this unit? Draw something that happened in the story. Tell your class about it.

D. Be a Disciple

1. *What Saint or holy person did you enjoy hearing about in this unit? Write the name here. Tell your class what this person did to follow Jesus.*

_____

\- \-

_____

2. *What can you do to be a good disciple of Jesus?*

_____

\- \-

_____

_____

\- \-

_____

The Last Supper

On the night before he died, Jesus ate a special meal with his Apostles. Here is what Jesus said and did.

Jesus took some bread. He gave thanks to God. He broke the bread. He shared the bread with his friends and said, "Eat this bread. It is my body."

Then Jesus took a cup filled with wine. He gave the cup to his friends and said, "Take this and drink. This is the cup of my blood. When you eat this bread and drink this wine, you remember me."

BASED ON 1 CORINTHIANS 11:23–26

What I Know

What is something you already know about these faith words?

Mary

_____

- -

_____

Holy Trinity

_____

- -

_____

Put an X next to the faith words you know.
Put a ? next to the faith words you need to learn more about.

____ angels	____ hope	____ Church
____ courage	____ Holy Spirit	____ Catholic

A Question I Have

What question would you like to ask about the Church?

_____

- -

_____

_____

- -

_____

CHAPTER 5

Mary, the Mother of Jesus

[?] What is your favorite family story?

In the Bible, we hear stories about Mary. Listen to what the angel Gabriel said to Mary:

Hail favored one! The Lord is with you.

BASED ON LUKE 1:28

[?] What do these words from the Bible tell you about God?

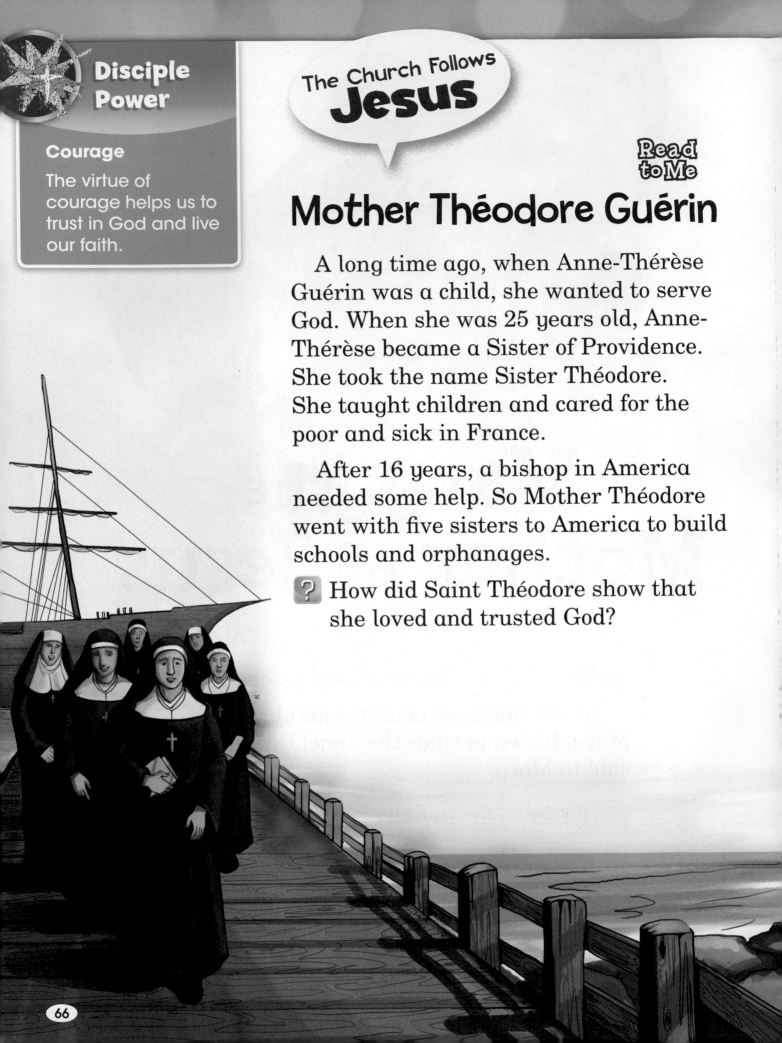

Disciple Power

Courage

The virtue of courage helps us to trust in God and live our faith.

The Church Follows
Jesus

Read to Me

Mother Théodore Guérin

A long time ago, when Anne-Thérèse Guérin was a child, she wanted to serve God. When she was 25 years old, Anne-Thérèse became a Sister of Providence. She took the name Sister Théodore. She taught children and cared for the poor and sick in France.

After 16 years, a bishop in America needed some help. So Mother Théodore went with five sisters to America to build schools and orphanages.

? How did Saint Théodore show that she loved and trusted God?

Trusting God

At first, Mother Théodore and the sisters were cold and lonely. But over the years, people learned to trust the sisters. Like Mary, Mother Théodore lived a life of service by helping people in need. She always trusted God.

The Church honors Mother Théodore Guérin as a Saint. The Church celebrates her feast day on October 3.

? How can you show that you love and trust God?

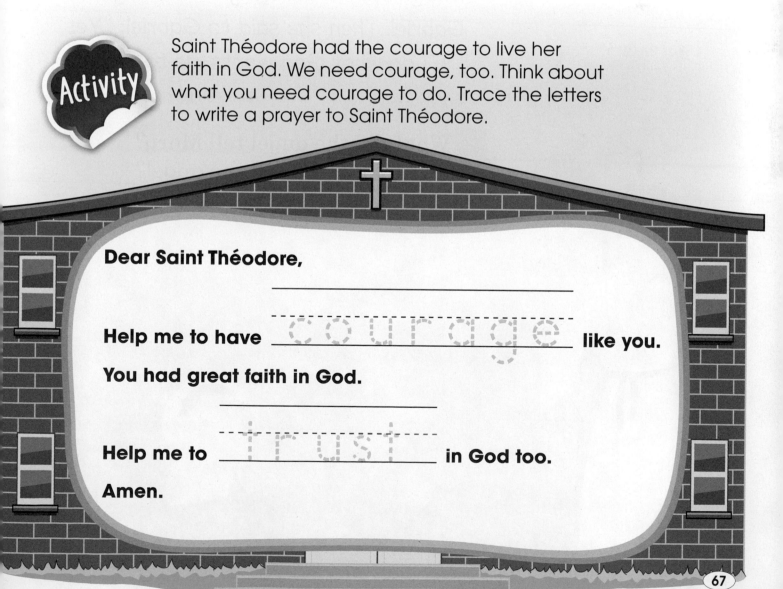

Activity Saint Théodore had the courage to live her faith in God. We need courage, too. Think about what you need courage to do. Trace the letters to write a prayer to Saint Théodore.

Dear Saint Théodore,

_____

Help me to have ___courage___ like you.

You had great faith in God.

_____

Help me to ___trust___ in God too.

Amen.

Faith Words
angels
Angels give honor and glory to God. They are God's messengers and helpers.

God Loves Mary

Angels are messengers of God. God sent the angel Gabriel to a young woman named Mary. The angel gave Mary this message from God. Gabriel said,

"You are blessed, Mary. The Holy Spirit will come to you. You will have a baby. The baby's name will be Jesus. He will be the Son of God."

Mary listened carefully to the angel Gabriel. Then she said to Gabriel, "Yes, I will do what God wants me to do."

BASED ON LUKE 1:28, 31, 35, 38

? **What did the angel tell Mary? What did Mary tell the angel?**

Mary Said, "Yes!"

Mary showed her love for God by saying, "Yes." Mary told Gabriel, "Yes, I will do what God wants me to do." God loves Mary.

? How does God show his love for you?

Activity

Showing Love for God

Talk with a partner about how the people in the pictures are saying yes to God. Draw one way you can say yes to God.

Catholics Believe

Feast Days

The Church honors and shows our love for Mary on special days each year. These are called feast days. Each year on September 8 we celebrate the Feast of the Nativity of the Blessed Virgin Mary. Another well-known feast of Mary is the Feast of Our Lady of Guadalupe, celebrated on December 12.

Faith Focus
What is trust?

Faith Words
▶ **trust**
To trust someone is to believe that person will always do what is best for us.

Say Yes to God

Mary listened carefully to the angel. She said yes to God. Mary had faith and **trust** in God. Mary loved God with her whole heart.

God asks us to have faith in him, too. God asks us to trust him and to love him with our whole heart.

? **What did Mary do to show her trust in God?**

Trust in God

We have faith and trust in God. We have faith that God will always be with us. We trust that God always loves us. We show we love God when we say yes to him as Mary did.

❓ How do you show trust in God?

Activity

Say Yes Every Day

Check (✓) ways you can say yes to God. I say yes to God when I

___ Pray every day.   ___ Share my toys.

___ Play fairly.   ___ Act mean.

___ Help at home.   ___ Say thank you.

Faith-Filled People

Saint Juan Diego

Juan Diego walked many miles to Mass every day. One day, our Blessed Mother Mary appeared to him on Tepeyac Hill. She told Juan that she wanted a church built on this site and sent him to talk to the bishop. Soon a church was built. People from all over the world visit Mary's special church.

God Chose Mary

God chose Mary to be the mother of Jesus. Jesus is God's Son. So we call Mary the Mother of God. Mary is very special.

Mary cared for Jesus. Jesus wants Mary to love and care for us too. He gave her to us as our special mother. Mary prays for us.

We celebrate Mary, the holy Mother of God on January 1. She prays to her son, Jesus, for us.

? Why is Mary our special mother?

Mary showed her faith and love for God. Courage can help you show your faith in God. You show your faith and love for God by what you say and what you do.

I Follow Jesus

Activity

I Trust in God

Choose one way you can show your courage as a follower of Jesus. Draw or write about it in this space.

My Faith Choice

This week, I will show my faith and love for God. I will

_____

- -

_____

Pray, "Thank you, God, for helping me to show my faith and love for you. Amen."

TO HELP YOU REMEMBER

1. God chose Mary to be the mother of Jesus.

2. The Bible tells us about Mary's faith in God.

3. Mary loves and trusts God.

Chapter Review

Recall

Complete the sentences. Color the circle next to the best choice.

1. Mary said, "____" to God.

○ Yes   ○ No

2. Courage helps us to ____ God.

○ trust   ○ know

3. When we trust someone we ____ the person will do what is best for us.

○ hope   ○ believe

4. Saint Juan Diego walked to ____ every day.

○ school   ○ Mass

5. God gave us Mary as our special ____.

○ mother   ○ friend

Reflect

Write a prayer to thank God for Mary.

_____

_____

_____

_____

Share   **Join with your class to pray one of the prayers you wrote to thank God.**

Psalm Prayer

Psalms are prayers in the Bible. We pray a psalm during Mass. Pray this prayer together.

Leader   We listen to God's Word, like Mary.

Jesus said, "Blessed are the people who hear the word of God and observe it."

BASED ON LUKE 11:28

All   **Happy are those who follow the law of the Lord!** Based on Psalm 1:1-2

Leader   We say yes to God, like Mary.

All   **Happy are those who follow the law of the Lord!**

Leader   We trust in God.

All   **Happy are those who follow the law of the Lord!**

Leader   We believe God cares for us.

All   **Happy are those who follow the law of the Lord!**

With My Family

This Week . . .

In Chapter 5, "Mary, the Mother of Jesus," your child learned:

▶ The Gospel account of the Annunciation tells us about the angel Gabriel announcing to Mary that God had chosen her to be the mother of Jesus.

▶ Mary is the mother of Jesus, the Son of God. Mary is the Mother of God.

▶ The Gospel account of the Annunciation shares with us Mary's faith and trust in God and her love for him.

▶ Courage helps us trust in God and live our faith, even in difficult times.

For more about related teachings of the Church, see the *Catechism of the Catholic Church*, 484–507, and the *United States Catholic Catechism for Adults*, pages 141–149.

■ Sharing God's Word

Read together Luke 1:26–38, the Gospel account of the Annunciation. Or read the adaptation of the story on page 68. Emphasize Mary's faith and trust in God and her love for him.

■ We Live as Disciples

The Christian home and family is a school of discipleship. Choose one or more of the following activities to do as a family, or design a similar activity of your own.

▶ Teach your child the Mass responses "Thanks be to God" and "Praise to you, Lord Jesus Christ." Guide your child to use these responses properly when your family takes part in the celebration of the Mass.

▶ Courage is the virtue that helps us trust God and live our faith. Help your child to recognize the ways your family is living this virtue. Remind them that when they say yes to God, they are living as a disciple of Jesus.

■ Our Spiritual Journey

The psalms are a profession of faith in song. From the time of David until the present, praying of the psalms has nourished the faith of the People of God. This prayer is both personal and communal. Memorize psalm verses such as the one on page 75 and pray them spontaneoulsy to respond to the various circiumstances of your life.

For more ideas on ways your family can live as disciples of Jesus, visit **BeMyDisciples.com**

CHAPTER 6

Jesus Shares God's Love

? How do family members show love for one another?

Jesus always shares God's love with people. He said,

"Let the children come to me. If you want to enter God's kingdom, become like a child." Then Jesus took the children in his arms and blessed them.

BASED ON MARK 10:14–16

? How do you show others that God loves them?

Hope

The virtue of hope helps us to remember that one day we may live in happiness with God forever in Heaven.

The Church Follows **Jesus**

Saint Gianna

Saint Gianna Beretta Molla was a wife, a mother, and a doctor. She cared for many people in her life. They all remembered her smile and her care for others.

Gianna believed that caring for the sick was one way to share God's love with others. If her patients did not have money to pay her, they paid her with eggs or chickens. Sometimes she paid for their medicine herself.

Gianna was a doctor who cared for children. She helped mothers learn how to take care of themselves and their children.

? Who are some of the people that share God's love with you?

Hope in God

Gianna wanted a family of her own. In 1955 she married Pietro Molla and soon they had three children. She helped them and all people have hope in God.

? Why is it important to have hope in God?

Gracias Thank You Danke Merci Cám on

Activity

Thank You Gracias Danke Merci

Sharing God's Love

Write a thank-you letter to a person who shares God's love with you.

_____

- - - - - - - - - - - - - - - - - - - -

Dear _____ ,

_____

- - - - - - - - - - - - - - - - - - - -

_____

_____

- - - - - - - - - - - - - - - - - - - -

_____

_____

- - - - - - - - - - - - - - - - - - - -

_____

_____

- - - - - - - - - - - - - - - - - - - -

_____

Thank you,

_____

- - - - - - - - - - - - - - - - - - - -

_____

Cám on Thank You Danke Gracias Merci Cám on

Merci Thank You Gracias Danke Merci

Jesus Loves Us

Jesus, the Son of God, always shared God's love with people. He helped people in many ways. Jesus forgave the people who hurt him.

Some people did not want Jesus to teach and help others. They had Jesus killed on a **cross**. This is called the Crucifixion.

Because he loved us so much, Jesus died on a cross for all of us. Jesus said,

"The greatest love is to give up your life for your friends."

BASED ON JOHN 15:13

❓ Why did Jesus die on the Cross?

Jesus Forgives Us

We are friends of Jesus. Because he loved us, Jesus died on a cross for all of us. Jesus forgave the people who put him on the Cross. He forgives us too.

Jesus forgives us when we sin. Jesus died so that we could live with him forever in Heaven.

? Why is it important to forgive one another?

Catholics Believe

Candlemas Day

Each year the Church blesses candles on February 2. This day is called Candlemas Day. We use these candles in our churches and in our homes. They remind us of the Risen Jesus, the Light of the world. We, too, are to be lights in the world.

Activity

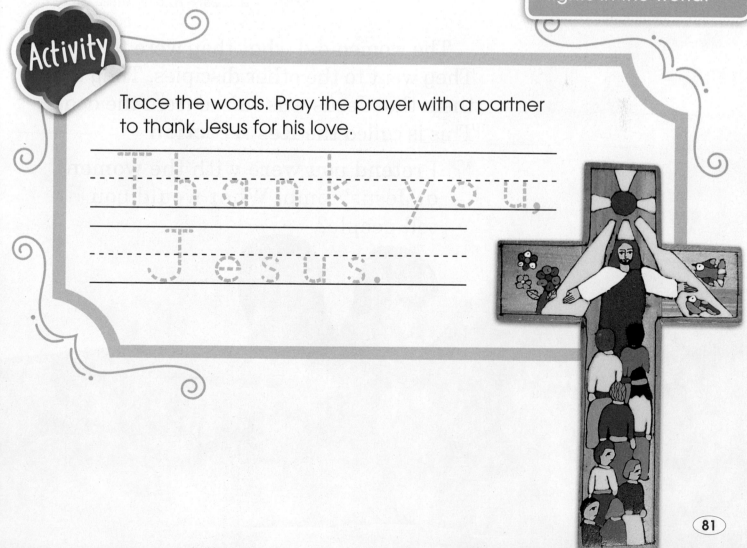

Trace the words. Pray the prayer with a partner to thank Jesus for his love.

Thank you,
Jesus.

Faith Focus
What happened to Jesus three days after he died?

Faith Words
Resurrection
God's raising Jesus from the dead to new life.

▶ **Easter**
Easter is the season when we celebrate that Jesus is risen.

Jesus Is Alive

After Jesus died on the Cross, his friends buried his body in a tomb. Three days later some women who were disciples, or followers, of Jesus went to the place where Jesus was buried. The women were very surprised at what they saw and heard. The Bible tells us,

The women came to the tomb. They saw two men in shining white robes. "Jesus is not here," the men said. "He has been raised from the dead. Go and tell the other disciples of Jesus."

BASED ON LUKE 24:1–4, 6; MATTHEW 28:6–7

The women did what they were told. They went to the other disciples. They told them that Jesus was raised from the dead. This is called the **Resurrection**.

❓ Pretend you were with the women at Jesus' tomb. What would you tell people?

Easter Celebrates New Life

We call the day of Jesus' Resurrection **Easter**. Easter celebrates the new life of Jesus. On the first Easter Sunday Jesus appeared to his disciples and said,

"Peace be with you."

JOHN 20:19

Easter celebrates the new life that Jesus gives us. We celebrate that Jesus is risen.

? How do you celebrate Easter at church and at home?

Faith-Filled People

Saint Mary Magdalene

Mary Magdalene was a disciple of Jesus. She was one of the women who went to the tomb. The women were the first ones to know that Jesus was raised from the dead. The Church celebrates the feast day of Saint Mary Magdalene on July 22.

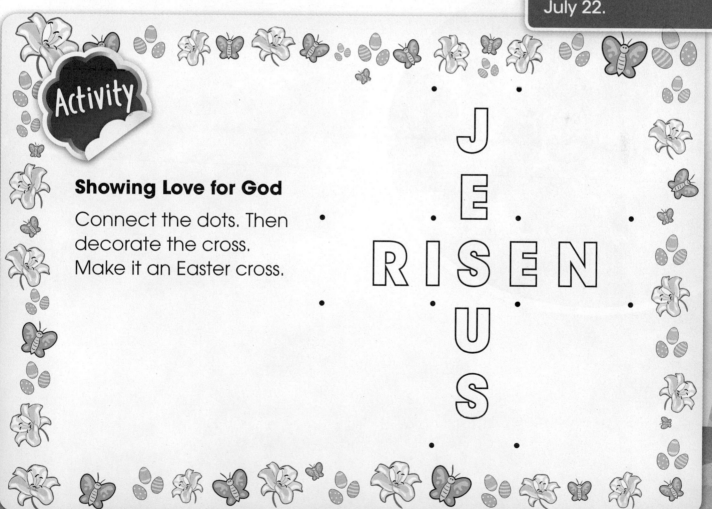

Activity

Showing Love for God

Connect the dots. Then decorate the cross. Make it an Easter cross.

J
E
R I S E N
U
S

Faith Focus
What do we call
Jesus' return to his
Father?

Faith Words
▶ **Ascension**
The Ascension of
Jesus is his return to
his Father in Heaven
after he was raised
from the dead.

Jesus Returned to His Father

After Jesus was raised from the dead, he stayed with his disciples for forty days. The Risen Jesus told his disciples to tell everyone in the world about him. Jesus told the disciples to invite everyone to believe in him and to be baptized.

Then Jesus returned to his Father in Heaven. We call this the **Ascension**. After we die, we hope that we too will return to God the Father in Heaven.

❓ What did the Risen Jesus ask his disciples to do?

The virtue of hope helps us to trust in God's love. When you tell others about Jesus, you are sharing God's love with people. You are a light in the world.

I Follow Jesus

Activity

Jesus Is Alive

Make a poster that tells people about Jesus. Use your poster as a reminder to act as a follower of Jesus.

My Faith Choice

This week, I will share my poster. I will tell someone about Jesus. I will say:

_____

- -

_____

Pray, "Thank you, Jesus, for teaching me how to be a light in the world. Amen."

Chapter Review

Recall

Draw lines from the words in Column A to the sentences that they complete in Column B.

Column A

1. forgives

2. raised

3. cross

4. Ascension

5. Easter

Column B

a. Jesus was _____ from the dead.

b. Jesus died on a _____ for all of us.

c. _____ celebrates Jesus being risen from the dead.

d. Jesus _____ us when we sin.

e. The _____ is Jesus' return to the Father in Heaven.

Reflect

Jesus lives today and you can talk to him at any time. Write what you would like to say to Jesus.

_____

- -

_____

- -

_____

Share Share your words with a partner and with your family at home.

An Act of Hope

The Church gives us a special prayer called the Act of Hope. In this prayer, we tell God we always trust in his love for us. His Word to us is always true. Pray this prayer together.

Leader

Let us pray.
O my God,
you always love us.
You are always good to us.
Your Word to us is always true.
With your help, we hope that
we will live with you in Heaven.
Amen.

All

(Sing to the tune "London Bridge.")
**Jesus came to show God's love,
Show God's love, show God's love.
Jesus came to show God's love.
Thank you, Jesus.**

**Jesus came to give us life,
Give us life, give us life.
Jesus came to give us life,
Life on Easter.**

**Jesus came to give us hope,
Give us hope, give us hope.
Jesus came to give us hope,
Hope for Heaven.**

With My Family

This Week . . .

In Chapter 6, "Jesus Shares God's Love," your child learned:

▶ Jesus showed his great love for us by dying on the Cross.

▶ Three days after his Death, Jesus was raised from the dead. Forty days later, Jesus ascended, or returned, to his Father in Heaven.

▶ Before he ascended to Heaven, Jesus commanded the disciples to evangelize the world. This means they were to tell all people about him and his teaching. They were to make disciples of all people and to baptize them.

▶ Hope is the virtue that helps us to remember and trust in God's love. We hope that one day we too will live in happiness with God forever in Heaven.

For more about related teachings of the Church, see the *Catechism of the Catholic Church*, 561, 620–621, 629, 656–665, and the *United States Catholic Catechism for Adults*, pages 77–87.

■ Sharing God's Word

Read together Luke 24:1–12, the account of the Resurrection. Or read the adaptation of the story on page 82. Emphasize that as the first disciples did, we are to tell people about Jesus.

■ We Live as Disciples

The Christian home and family is a school of discipleship. Choose one or more of the following activities to do as a family, or design a similar activity of your own.

▶ Jesus tells us that we are to be lights in the world. Each night at dinner, light a candle as part of your mealtime prayer. Take turns telling about how each family member was a light in the world that day.

▶ It is difficult to know everyone in your school or parish. Each month make an effort to introduce yourselves as a family to one new family in your school or parish.

■ Our Spiritual Journey

Our spiritual pilgrimage is a journey of hope. It is with confidence that we trust that God's promise of eternal life will come true. Learn, and help your child learn, An Act of Hope. Pray it regularly. You can use the prayer on page 87.

For more ideas on ways your family can live as disciples of Jesus, visit **BeMyDisciples.com**

CHAPTER 7

The Holy Spirit, Our Helper

? Who are some of the people who help you to learn new things?

Everyone needs teachers and helpers. The Holy Spirit is the special teacher and helper Jesus sent to us.

Jesus told his disciples, "God, my Father, will send you the Holy Spirit. The Holy Spirit will be your helper." BASED ON JOHN 14:26

? What do you know about the Holy Spirit?

Disciple Power

Counsel

Counsel is another word for the help that the Holy Spirit gives us. Counsel is a Gift of the Holy Spirit. This gift helps us choose to live as followers of Jesus.

Signs of the Holy Spirit

We learn about God in many different ways through words and pictures. Some churches have colorful stained-glass windows. They may show pictures of Jesus, Mary, and the other Saints.

Sometimes these windows have special pictures, or symbols, of the Holy Spirit. Flames of fire and a white dove are two symbols of the Holy Spirit.

The light shining through stained-glass windows reminds us of God's love for us. The Holy Spirit helps us to share that love with others.

? What are some symbols of the Holy Spirit that you see in your church?

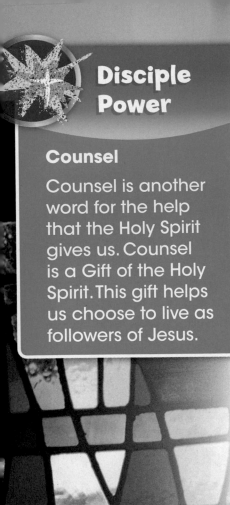

Sharing God's Love

God loves each of us. We share that love with others. The Holy Spirit helps us to share God's love.

? What is one way you share God's love with your family?

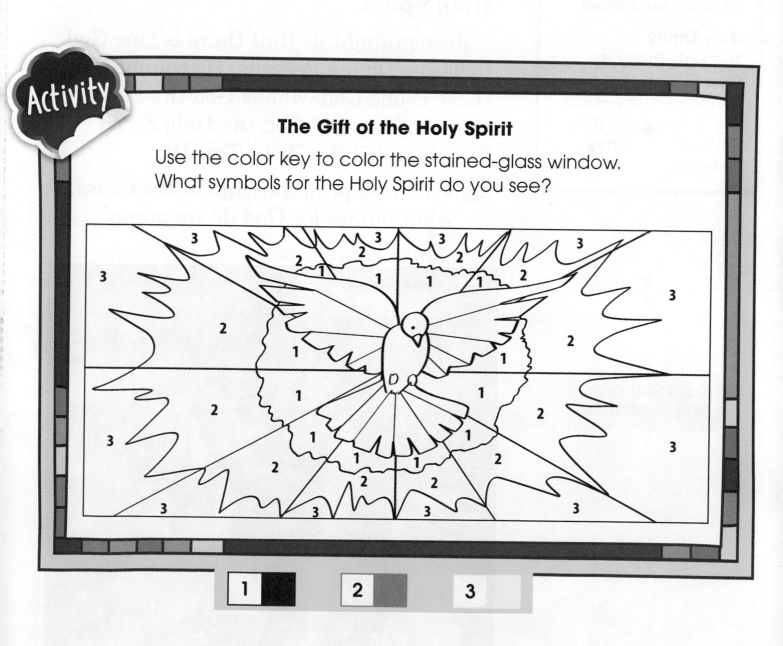

Activity

The Gift of the Holy Spirit

Use the color key to color the stained-glass window. What symbols for the Holy Spirit do you see?

1   2   3

Faith Words

Holy Spirit
The Holy Spirit is the Third Person of the Holy Trinity. The Holy Spirit is always with us to be our helper.

Holy Trinity
The Holy Trinity is One God in Three Divine Persons—God the Father, God the Son, and God the Holy Spirit.

The Holy Spirit Is with Us

Jesus taught us that there is only one God. Jesus is the Son of God. Jesus is true God and true man. He taught us about God the Father and God the **Holy Spirit**.

Jesus taught us that there is One God in Three Divine Persons. He taught that there is one God, who is God the Father, God the Son, and God the Holy Spirit. This is called the **Holy Trinity**.

❓ When we pray the Sign of the Cross, what names for God do we name?

Saint Patrick, patron of Ireland

Praying the Sign of the Cross

Sometimes we pray the Sign of the Cross and bless ourselves. Praying the Sign of the Cross shows that we believe in the Holy Trinity.

? When do we pray the Sign of the Cross?

Faith-Filled People

Saint Patrick

Patrick was a bishop. He taught people in Ireland about the Holy Trinity. The Church celebrates the feast day of Saint Patrick on March 17.

Activity

Three Persons in One God

A shamrock helps us remember that there are Three Persons in One God. Trace the names of these Persons in the leaves.

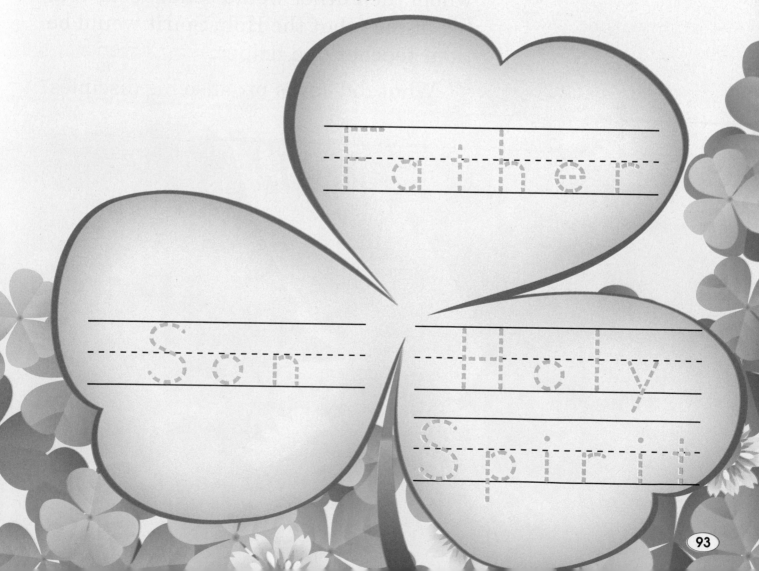

Father

Son

Holy Spirit

93

Jesus' Promise

Jesus told his disciples that he was going to leave them and return to the Father. When Jesus' disciples heard this, they felt sad. He made a promise to his friends.

He promised that God the Father would send them a helper. Jesus said,

"The Father will give you a helper who will be with you always."

BASED ON JOHN 14:16

God the Holy Spirit is the helper whom the Father would send. Jesus told his friends that the Holy Spirit would be their teacher and helper.

❓ What did Jesus promise his disciples?

Teacher and Helper

The Holy Spirit would teach and help the disciples to understand what Jesus said and did. The Holy Spirit would teach and help them to live as Jesus' friends and followers.

The Holy Spirit is our teacher and helper too. The Holy Spirit helps us to live as Jesus' followers.

? What are the ways the Holy Spirit helps us?

Catholics Believe

Signs and Symbols

Signs and symbols help us to understand the meaning of what God has told us. The Church uses a beautiful white dove as a sign of the Holy Spirit.

Activity

Loving Others

In each box, write the number of the picture that matches the sentence.

☐ I help my community.

☐ I help my family.

☐ I say my prayers.

The Gift of the Holy Spirit

The Holy Spirit is the Third Person of the Holy Trinity. We first receive the gift of the Holy Spirit at Baptism. The Holy Spirit is our helper. The Holy Spirit is always with us.

The Holy Spirit teaches us to pray. The Holy Spirit helps us learn what Jesus told his followers.

Love one another as I love you.

BASED ON JOHN 13:34

The Holy Spirit helps and teaches us to love God and one another.

? What are the ways that you show love to others?

God the Holy Spirit is always with you. The Holy Spirit is your helper and teacher. The Holy Spirit helps you to make good choices to live as a follower of Jesus.

I Follow Jesus

Activity

Teach Me to Love

Draw the Holy Spirit helping you show love.

My Faith Choice

This week, I will remember to do what I drew about.

Pray, "Thank you, Holy Spirit, for helping me to show my love as Jesus taught. Amen."

TO HELP YOU REMEMBER

1. The Holy Spirit helps and teaches us to pray.

2. The Holy Spirit helps us to know what Jesus taught.

3. The Holy Spirit helps and teaches us to do what Jesus asked us to do.

Chapter Review

Recall

Complete the sentences. Circle the best word.

1. God the Father, Son, and Holy Spirit is the Holy _____.

   Family　　　**Trinity**　　　**Bible**

2. The Holy Spirit is our _____.

   father　　　**brother**　　　**helper**

3. The Holy Spirit's gift of _____ helps us choose to live as disciples of Jesus.

   counsel　　　**thinking**　　　**joy**

Reflect

Find and circle the names in the puzzle. Think about what each name tells you about God.

Father	Son	Holy Spirit

```
Q  F  A  T  H  E  R
W  S  O  N  E  O  P
H  O  L  Y  C  M  S
L  S  P  I  R  I  T
```

Share Share with your class what you believe each name tells you about God.

Come, Holy Spirit

Learn this prayer to the Holy Spirit. Pray it together. Use gestures to pray.

**Come,
Holy Spirit,
fill our hearts with
the fire of
your love.
Amen.**

Leader   Let us listen to God's Word.

Reader   *For those who are led by the Spirit of God are children of God.*

ROMANS 8:14

The word of the Lord.

All   **Thanks be to God.**

Leader   Come, Holy Spirit, help us to listen to you.

All   **Come Holy Spirit, lead us.**

Leader   Come, Holy Spirit, help us to make good choices.

All   **Come Holy Spirit, lead us.
Amen.**

With My Family

This Week . . .

In Chapter 7, "The Holy Spirit, Our Helper," your child learned:

▶ The Holy Trinity is the mystery of One God in Three Divine Persons. Before Jesus died, he promised the disciples that he would not leave them alone and that the Father would send them the Advocate.

▶ The Holy Spirit is the Advocate whom the Father sent and who is always with us. The Holy Spirit helps us to know, believe, and live what Jesus taught.

▶ Counsel is a Gift of the Holy Spirit that helps us to make wise decisions to live as Jesus taught.

For more about related teachings of the Church, see the *Catechism of the Catholic Church,* 232–248 and 683–741, and the *United States Catholic Catechism for Adults,* pages 101–110.

■ Sharing God's Word

Read together John 14:26 or the adaptation on page 94. Emphasize that the Holy Spirit, the Advocate, is always with us to live as Jesus taught.

■ We Live as Disciples

The Christian home and family is a school of discipleship. Choose one or more of the following activities to do as a family, or design a similar activity of your own.

▶ Make prayer cards, using the Prayer to the Holy Spirit on page 99. Decorate the cards with signs and symbols of the Holy Spirit. Keep the cards where they will serve as reminders that the Holy Spirit is always with your family as your teacher and helper.

▶ This week, your child learned about the Holy Trinity. Now is a good time to review the Sign of the Cross with your child. Talk about how the Sign of the Cross names all Three Persons of the Holy Trinity.

■ Our Spiritual Journey

To give counsel is one of the Spiritual Works of Mercy. Make the Holy Spirit the center of your decision-making process. and teach your child to do the same. Teach your child to respect the counsel of trusted adults, such as parents, teachers, and older family members. In this chapter, your child learned a prayer to the Holy Spirit. Read and pray together the prayer on page 99.

For more ideas on ways your family can live as disciples of Jesus, visit **BeMyDisciples.com**

CHAPTER 8

The Church

? What do you do together as a family?

Each of us belongs to a family. We also belong to the family of the Church. The Bible tells us:

> The first members of the Church spent time together. They remembered Jesus. They shared all they had with one another. They prayed together. They broke and shared bread together. Together they praised God

BASED ON ACTS OF THE APOSTLES 2:42

? What does your family do at church?

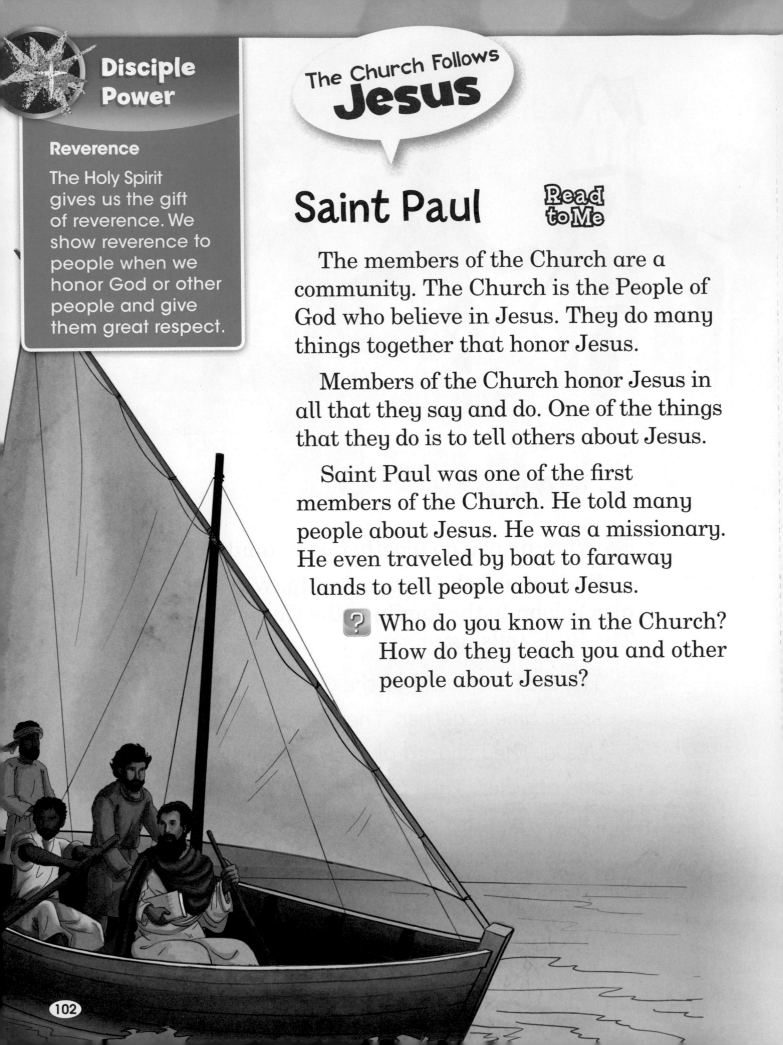

Reverence

The Holy Spirit gives us the gift of reverence. We show reverence to people when we honor God or other people and give them great respect.

The Church Follows Jesus

Saint Paul

Read to Me

The members of the Church are a community. The Church is the People of God who believe in Jesus. They do many things together that honor Jesus.

Members of the Church honor Jesus in all that they say and do. One of the things that they do is to tell others about Jesus.

Saint Paul was one of the first members of the Church. He told many people about Jesus. He was a missionary. He even traveled by boat to faraway lands to tell people about Jesus.

? Who do you know in the Church? How do they teach you and other people about Jesus?

Tell the Good News

Today, the Church tells people all over the world about Jesus Christ, just as Saint Paul did. We show reverence for Saint Paul and all holy people.

? How do you honor Jesus?

Activity

Honoring Jesus

In each box, write the number of the picture that best matches the sentence.

☐ This member of our Church family honors Jesus by leading us in worship.

☐ This member of our Church family honors Jesus by teaching us about him.

☐ This member of our Church family honors Jesus by caring for people in need.

☐ This member of our Church family honors Jesus by sharing God's Word with us.

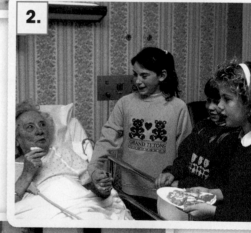

1.

2.

3.

4.

Our Church Family

Faith Focus
Who helps us to live
as followers of Jesus?

Faith Words
Church
The Church is the
People of God who
believe in Jesus and
live as his followers.

Pentecost
Pentecost is the
day the Holy Spirit
came to Jesus'
disciples and the
Church began.

The People of God who believe in Jesus and live as his followers are called the **Church**. The Holy Spirit helps the Church to live as followers or disciples of Jesus.

After the Risen Jesus returned to his Father in Heaven, the disciples went to the city of Jerusalem. They were in a room in a house. The Holy Spirit came to them as Jesus promised.

Read what happened:

The disciples of Jesus heard a sound like a strong wind. Small flames settled over each person's head. The power of the Holy Spirit filled the disciples of Jesus.

BASED ON ACTS OF THE APOSTLES 2:1–4

❓ What happened to the disciples of Jesus in the room?

The Church Begins

The day that the Holy Spirit came to the disciples is called **Pentecost**. This day was the start of the Church. Peter the Apostle and all the other disciples began to do the work Jesus gave them to do. They told people about Jesus. They invited people to be baptized. The work of the Church began.

? What is the work of the Church?

Faith-Filled People

Saint Peter the Apostle

Peter the Apostle was one of the first disciples of Jesus. Jesus chose Peter to be the first leader of the whole Church. The Church celebrates the feast day of Saints Peter and Paul on June 29.

Activity

Celebrating the Church

Use the words in the flames to finish a poem about the Church.

Pentecost   **Disciples**   **Spirit**   **Church**

_____

The **C** _____ celebrates special days for you and me.

P _____ is one of those days, you see.

We celebrate how the Holy **S** _____ came.

And the **D** _____ went out to spread Jesus' name.

Faith Focus
What do members of
the Church do?

Faith Words
Catholics
Catholics are
followers of Jesus
and members of the
Catholic Church.

We Are Catholics

The Catholic Church goes all the way back to Jesus and the Apostles. We belong to the Catholic Church. The Pope is the leader of the Catholic Church.

We join the Church when we are baptized. **Catholics** are followers of Jesus Christ. We do what Jesus taught us. We believe in him. We learn about God and his love for us.

We teach others about Jesus. We help people who are poor, sick, hungry, or in need. We pray together. We share our love for Jesus with one another.

? Who are Catholics? What do Catholics do?

Pope Francis

The Catholic Church

The Catholic Church teaches us about Jesus. The Church helps us to live as followers of Jesus. The same Holy Spirit who came on Pentecost is with the Church today. The Holy Spirit helps the Church guide us and teach us.

❓ What does the Catholic Church do?

Catholics Believe

The Pope

The Pope is the leader of the whole Catholic Church. The Pope helps us to live as followers of Jesus.

About the Church

Find the letter that goes with each number.
Write the letter on the line above the number.
Find out three things that Catholics do.

A	B	C	D	E	F	G	H	I	J	K	L	M
1	2	3	4	5	6	7	8	9	10	11	12	13
N	O	P	Q	R	S	T	U	V	W	X	Y	Z
14	15	16	17	18	19	20	21	22	23	24	25	26

____ ____ ____ ____ ____
12   5   1   18   14

____ ____ ____ ____
16   18   1   25

____ ____ ____ ____
8   5   12   16

Faith Focus
Who are the Saints?

Faith Words
Saints
Saints are people who live with God forever in Heaven.

The Saints

Members of our Church show us how to live as followers of Jesus. Some of these people are called **Saints**. Saints are grown-ups and children from all over the world. The Church has named many Saints.

Mary, Mother of Jesus, is the greatest Saint of all. We can pray to Mary and the other Saints.

All of the Saints want to help us to live as children of God. They want us to live as followers of Jesus. They want us to be happy with God on Earth and in Heaven.

? Who shows you how to live as a child of God? How do they show you?

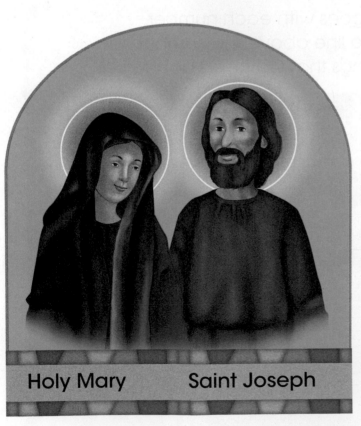

Holy Mary   Saint Joseph

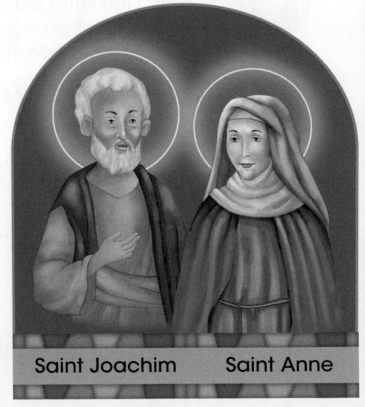

Saint Joachim   Saint Anne

The Holy Spirit gives you the gift of reverence. This gift helps you to honor God. You honor God when you serve him and others as Jesus taught. You show that you are a good Catholic.

I Follow Jesus

Activity

Honoring God and Others

In one footstep, show how you will honor God. In the other footstep, show how you will honor others.

My Faith Choice

I can show reverence to God and others. This week, I will do what I drew in the footsteps above.

Pray, "Thank you, God, for helping me to show that I belong to the Catholic Church. Amen."

1. The Holy Spirit helps all members of the Church.

2. The Church helps us do what Jesus taught us.

3. The Saints help us live as followers of Jesus.

Chapter Review

Recall

Color the circle next to the word that best completes each sentence.

1. The _____ came to Jesus' followers on Pentecost.

   ○ Holy Trinity   ○ Holy Spirit

2. _____ is the greatest Saint.

   ○ Peter   ○ Mary

3. Paul told people about _____.

   ○ Jesus   ○ Mary

4. At _____ we became members of the Church.

   ○ Pentecost   ○ Baptism

5. The Pope is the leader of the _____ Church.

   ○ Catholic   ○ Communion

Reflect

Write the name of someone who taught you how to live as a follower of Jesus.

_____

- -

_____

Share **What did this person teach you? Share it with a classmate.**

Litany of the Saints

We praise and thank God for the Saints in a litany prayer. Pray together.

Reader   Holy Mary, Mother of God,

All   **pray for us.**

Reader   Saint Paul,

All   **pray for us.**

Reader   Saint Anne, mother of Mary,

All   **pray for us.**

Reader   Saint Peter,

All   **pray for us.**

Reader   All holy men and women,

All   **pray for us.**

All   **Saints of God, for us, please pray.
Help us grow in faith each day.
Help us love and care a lot.
Help us do what Jesus taught.
Amen.**

With My Family

This Week . . .

In Chapter 8, "The Church," your child learned:

▶ The Church began on Pentecost. On Pentecost, the Holy Spirit came upon the disciples, and they received the power to go out and preach to others about Jesus. The work that Jesus gave to the Church began.

▶ God has called us together in Christ to be his Church, the new People of God. Christ is the head of the Church, the Body of Christ. We are members of the Church. We believe in Jesus Christ and in everything he revealed to us.

▶ We work together as the Body of Christ to share our love for Jesus with others. The Saints provide us with examples of how to live as disciples of Jesus Christ in the world today.

▶ The Holy Spirit gives us the gift of reverence. This gift inspires us to honor God by serving him and others.

For more about related teachings of the Church, see the *Catechism of the Catholic Church*, 737–741 and 748–801, and the *United States Catholic Catechism for Adults*, pages 111–123.

■ Sharing God's Word

Read together the Bible story in Acts 2:1–41 about Pentecost or read the adaptation of the story on page 104. Emphasize that on Pentecost the Holy Spirit came to the disciples, and the disciples began the work of the Church.

■ We Live as Disciples

The Christian home and family is a school of discipleship. Choose one or more of the following activities to do as a family, or design a similar activity of your own.

▶ Identify and name ways that you live as members of the Catholic Church. For example, we take part in Mass, we help the poor and hungry, and we help a neighbor in need, or we visit the sick.

▶ The Saints show us how to live as followers of Jesus. If your parish is named after a Saint, take time this week to find out more about the Saint. Talk about how this Saint or another Saint, if your parish is not named after a Saint, helps you live as a Christian family.

■ Our Spiritual Journey

The Church is the Communion of Saints. When we die, our lives are changed but not ended. The Saints of the Church are our companions on our earthly journey. In this chapter, your child prayed part of the Litany of the Saints. Read and pray together the prayer on page 111. Or pray your own Litany of Saints as a family each day this week. Begin with *"Holy Mary Mother of God . . . pray for us."* Then add the names of family members' favorite Saints to the litany.

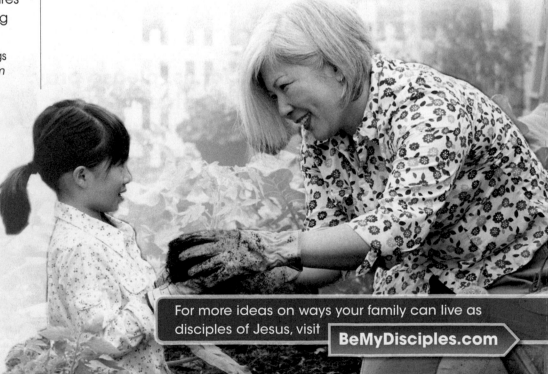

For more ideas on ways your family can live as disciples of Jesus, visit **BeMyDisciples.com**

No Place to Live

The fire was a big story on the news. An old house across town had burned down. The family who lived there got out of the house in time.

The three children are scared and sad. The children's parents, who have no jobs, are very worried. The family has little money, few clothes, no food, and now, no place to live.

Christmas is coming soon, and there are no presents for the children. The family needs your help.

WE CARE FOR PEOPLE

Christians help people who have special needs. We can help people who need food, clothes, and a place to live.

Making Connections

Followers of Jesus help people who are in need. What can you do to help people in need such as the family who lost their home in the fire?

with SOCIAL STUDIES

Your class will collect clothes and toys for the family who lost their home in the fire. Think about the place where you live. What is the weather like? What kind of clothes does the family need? What kinds of toys would be best? Make a list.

with MATH AND SCIENCE

The family is coming to visit with your class at 1:30. Draw a clock that has the time 1:30. Draw a clock at 1:00. You have time to clean your classroom before the family visits.

with LANGUAGE ARTS

Create a poster that shows you want to help people in need. Finish this sentence with a word that rhymes with the word "care."

To show we care, we _____.
Use the saying on your poster.

Faith Action

What is one way you can show people you care? Tell your class.

_____

_____

_____

Unit 2 Review

A. Choose the Best Word

Complete the sentences. Color the circle next to the best choice.

1. God chose _____ to be the Mother of Jesus.

   ○ Gabriel   ○ Mary

2. Jesus _____ us so much that he gave his life for us.

   ○ loved   ○ missed

3. Jesus returned to his Father in _____.

   ○ Heaven   ○ Nazareth

4. The _____ helps and teaches us to pray.

   ○ Creator   ○ Holy Spirit

5. The _____ of the Church help us to live as followers of Jesus.

   ○ Saints   ○ angels

B. Show What You Know

Circle the numbers next to the words that tell about the Holy Trinity.

1. God the Father   4. the Holy Spirit

2. Mary, the Mother of God   5. the People of God

3. Jesus the Son   6. the Saints

C. Connect with Scripture

What was your favorite story about Jesus in this unit? Draw something that happened in the story. Tell your class about it.

D. Be a Disciple

1. *What Saint or holy person did you enjoy hearing about in this unit? Write the name here. Tell your class what this person did to follow Jesus.*

_____

- -

_____

2. *What can you do to be a good disciple of Jesus?*

_____

- -

_____

_____

- -

_____

Come, Follow Me

Jesus looked out on the water and saw Simon and Andrew fishing. He called to them, "Come, follow me. I will teach you how to catch people, instead of fish."

The two brothers said, "Yes!" Off they went to follow Jesus.

Soon, Jesus spied two more fishermen named James and John. They were fixing their fishing nets.

"Come, follow me," Jesus said. The brothers said, "Yes!" Off they went to follow Jesus.

BASED ON MARK 1:16–20

What I Know

What is something you already know about these faith words?

Easter

_____

- -

_____

Baptism

_____

- -

_____

Put an X next to the faith words you know.
Put a ? next to the faith words you need to learn more about.

____ Easter   ____ godparents   ____ marriage

____ Sacraments   ____ Gospel   ____ goodness

A Question I Have

What question would you like to ask about the Sacraments?

_____

- -

_____

_____

- -

_____

CHAPTER 9

The Church Celebrates Jesus

? What is your favorite season, or time, of the year?

The Church has seasons too. Let us listen to what the Bible tells us about the seasons of the year. In the Bible, God tells us:

> There is a season for everything.
> There is a time of the year for everything.
>
> BASED ON ECCLESIASTES 3:1

? What is your favorite time of the year that you celebrate with the Church?

Prudence

Prudence helps us ask advice from others when making important decisions. A prudent person makes good choices. Our Church family helps us to make good choices.

The Church Follows **Jesus**

Celebrating Sunday

Sunday is the Lord's Day. Maya Lopez and her family celebrate the Church year every Sunday. The Lopez family keep Sunday holy in many ways.

Maya and her family gather with their Church family for Mass. Every Sunday they remember that Jesus was raised from the dead.

Sunday is a special family day too. Maya's family spends time together. Sometimes they visit relatives. Sometimes they gather for a special dinner. They celebrate that their family is part of God's family.

❓ How does your family celebrate Sunday, the Lord's Day?

Activity

Family Celebrations

Look at the pictures. Write next to each picture how the people are celebrating Sunday, the Lord's Day. Then, draw and write about one way your family celebrates Sunday, the Lord's Day.

_____

_____

_____

_____

_____

_____

_____

_____

_____

Faith Words

Church year
The Church year is made up of seasons. They are Advent, Christmas, Lent, and Easter.

Advent
Advent is the first season of the Church year. We prepare for Christmas and get our hearts ready for Jesus.

The Seasons of the Church Year

The different times of the **Church year** are called its seasons. Each season of the Church year tells us something about Jesus. All year long we remember God's love for us.

Advent, Christmas, Lent, Easter, and Ordinary Time are the seasons and times of the Church year. Each season of the Church year has its own color. This helps us to remember which season of the Church year we are celebrating.

❓ Look at the pictures. What are the names of these seasons and times of the Church year?

Advent

Advent is the first season of the Church year. During Advent, we prepare the way of the Lord. We get our hearts ready for Jesus. The Bible says:

> Prepare the way of the LORD. Make his path straight. The LORD is coming in glory for all people to see.
>
> BASED ON ISAIAH 40:3, 5

The Advent season is four weeks long. The color for Advent is purple. The Advent wreath reminds us to prepare for Christmas each week.

? What are the ways that your school, parish, or family uses the Advent wreath to celebrate Advent?

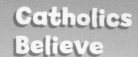
Holy Days of Obligation

In addition to Sunday, Catholics have the responsibility to take part in Mass on other days. These days are called holy days of obligation.

Activity

Color three candles purple and one candle pink in the Advent wreath.

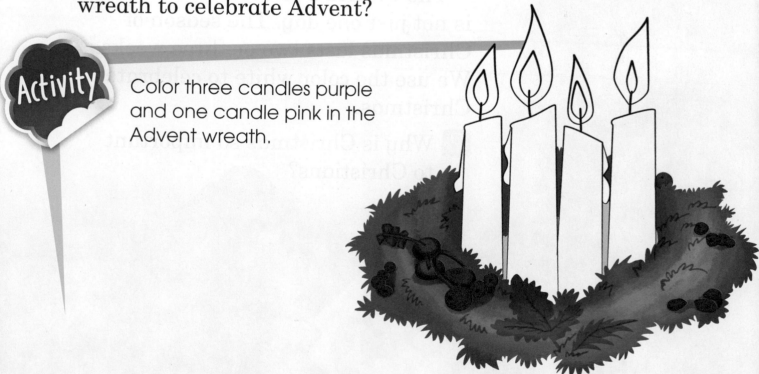

Faith Focus
What do we celebrate during the seasons of Christmas, Lent and Easter?

Faith Words
▶ **Easter**
Easter is a season of the Church year. It is the time of the year when we celebrate that Jesus was raised from the dead.

Christmas

Christmas comes after Advent. During the Christmas season we remember the birth of Jesus in Bethlehem. Here is what the Bible says:

O little town of Bethlehem, a great ruler shall come from you. He will care for God's people like a good shepard. The whole world will know about him. He shall be peace.

BASED ON MICAH 5:1, 3–4

Jesus is God's Son who came to live on Earth with us. Jesus is God's greatest gift to us.

The Church's celebration of Christmas is not just one day. The season of Christmas lasts two or three weeks. We use the color white to celebrate Christmas.

❓ Why is Christmas so important to Christians?

Lent

During Lent we remember that Jesus died for us on the Cross. We also get ready for Easter. The season of Lent begins on Ash Wednesday and lasts forty days. The color for Lent is purple.

Easter

During the season of **Easter** we celebrate that Jesus was raised from the dead. This is the most important celebration of the whole Church year. It is a time of great joy. The season of Easter lasts seven weeks. The Easter candle is lighted to remind us that Jesus is risen. The color for Easter is white.

? What are the ways your school, parish, or family celebrate Christmas and Easter?

Faith-Filled People

Saint Joseph

Joseph was the husband of Mary and the foster father of Jesus. An angel told Joseph that Mary was going to have a baby. An angel told Mary and Joseph to give the baby the name Jesus. The Church celebrates Saint Joseph, Spouse of the Blessed Virgin Mary, on March 19.

Activity

Color the Seasons

Color the symbols for Christmas, Lent, and Easter.

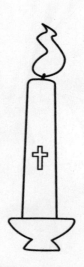

Ordinary Time

Ordinary Time is the longest part of the Church year. During Ordinary Time we listen to Bible stories about what Jesus said and did. We listen to his teachings. We listen to what he told us about God. We learn how he helped people. We learn to be followers of Jesus.

Jesus said,

"I am the good shepherd, and I know mine and mine know me, . . .

My sheep hear my voice;
I know them, and they follow me."

JOHN 10:14, 27

The color for Ordinary Time is green. Ordinary Time is our time to become better followers of Jesus.

? What is your favorite story about Jesus? Why is this your favorite story?

When you celebrate the Church's seasons, you are making a good choice. Prudence helps you to make that good choice and others too.

I Follow Jesus

Activity

Celebrating Jesus All Year

Look at the picture. Which season of the Church year does it show?

_____

- - - - - - - - - - - - - - - - - - -

_____

My Faith Choice

I will, celebrate the season of the Church year that we are in right now. I will

_____

- - - - - - - - - - - - - - - - - - -

_____.

Pray, "Thank you, Holy Spirit, for helping me to celebrate the Church year. Amen."

1. The Church has special times, or seasons, of the year.

2. The Church year is made up of Advent, Christmas, Lent, Easter, and Ordinary Time.

3. Sunday is the Lord's Day.

Chapter Review

Recall

Draw lines to match the Church seasons with what we celebrate.

Season	What We Celebrate
Easter	We get ready for Easter.
Christmas	We celebrate that Jesus was raised from the dead.
Lent	We get ready for Christmas.
Advent	We remember the birth of Jesus.

For each season of the Church year, write in the correct color—P for purple, W for white, or G for Green.

Advent   _____

Christmas   _____

Lent   _____

Easter   _____

Ordinary Time   _____

Reflect

How do the colors of the Church year help you to celebrate Jesus?

_____

- -

_____

Share   **Tell a partner why the colors of the Church year are important.**

Lord, We Praise You

When we worship God, we tell him that only he is God. Pray this prayer of praise together.

Group 1   In the morning and the night,

All   **Lord, we praise you.**

Group 2   In the summer and the fall,

All   **Lord, we praise you.**

Group 1   In the winter and the spring,

All   **Lord, we praise you.**

Group 2   Every day of the year,

All   **Lord, we praise you.**

Leader   God our loving Father, we praise you for the seasons of the year. All year long, you share your goodness and love with us. We praise you for Jesus Christ, your Son, and for the Holy Spirit.

All   **Amen.**

With My Family

This Week . . .

In Chapter 9, "The Church Celebrates Jesus," your child learned:

▶ The Church year has special seasons just as the calendar year has. The seasons and times of the Church year are Advent, Christmas, Lent, Easter, and Ordinary Time.

▶ Sunday is the Lord's Day.

▶ During the Church year we join with Christ all year long and share in his work of Salvation. All year long we give thanks and praise to God.

▶ The virtue of prudence helps us to consistently make good choices. This includes taking part in Mass on Sunday.

For more about related teachings of the Church, see the *Catechism of the Catholic Church*, 1163–1173, and the *United States Catholic Catechism for Adults*, pages 173, 175, 178.

■ Sharing God's Word

Read together Psalm 150. Emphasize that all throughout the liturgical year, the Church gives praise and thanks to God. Talk about the ways in which your family is already giving thanks and praise to God.

■ We Live as Disciples

The Christian home and family is a school of discipleship. Choose one or more of the following activities to do as a family, or design a similar activity of your own.

▶ When you take part in Mass this weekend, look around and listen for all the signs that tell you what season of the Church year the Church is now celebrating. Point them out to your child and talk about them with him or her.

▶ Choose an activity that helps you celebrate the current liturgical season as a family at home. For example, during Advent you might use an Advent wreath or an Advent calendar to help anticipate and prepare for Christmas.

■ Our Spiritual Journey

Praising God is one of the five main forms of prayer that are part of the tradition of God's people. In this chapter, your child prayed a prayer of praise on page 129. Pray this version of a prayer of praise as a family.

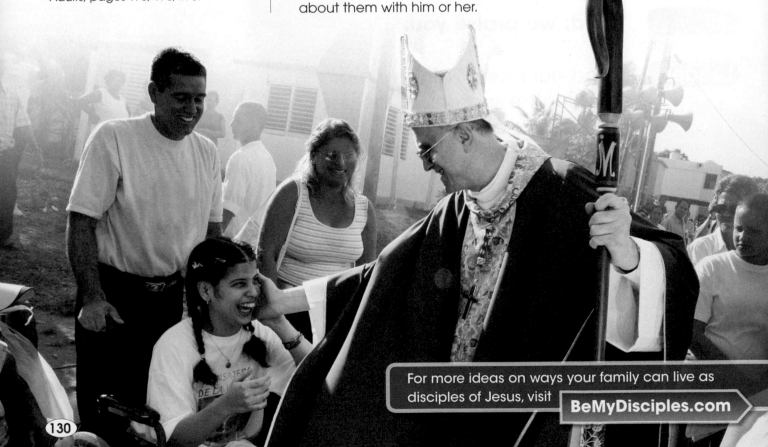

For more ideas on ways your family can live as disciples of Jesus, visit **BeMyDisciples.com**

CHAPTER 10

Signs of God's Love

? What special days and times does your family celebrate?

The Bible tells us about a time Jesus took part in a special celebration. John the Baptist baptized Jesus in the Jordan River.

As Jesus came up out of the water, he saw the clouds disappear. The Holy Spirit, like a dove, came down upon him. A voice from the sky said, "You are my Son, the One I love."

BASED ON MARK 1:10–11

? Why does God the Father love Jesus so much?

Hospitality

We demonstrate hospitality when we welcome others as God's children. We show that we respect others.

The Church Follows **Jesus**

Project Star Fish Read to Me

One day, the first-grade children at Divine Redeemer School in Colorado were learning about Baptism with their teacher, Mrs. Murphy. She asked the class, "What do you see happen at a Baptism?"

Carter raised his hand. "The priest pours water on the baby," he said.

Bella said, "The baby gets a candle."

Mrs. Murphy explained, "Yes, at your Baptism you were given a lighted candle too. This candle is called a baptismal candle. The candle reminds us that Jesus told us to be lights in the world. When we live our Baptism, we are lights in the world."

? What can you do to be a light in the world?

Lights In the World

Mrs. Murphy's class wanted to be lights in the world. They started Project Star Fish. In this project, they share God's love with children who have no families.

Students gather clothing, toys, and school supplies. They share these things with children living in the country of Jamaica. The children of Divine Redeemer School are bright lights for the children of Jamaica.

? What can your class do to be lights in the world?

Activity On each leg of the starfish, write one way we can show hospitality and be lights for others. Then color the starfish a bright color.

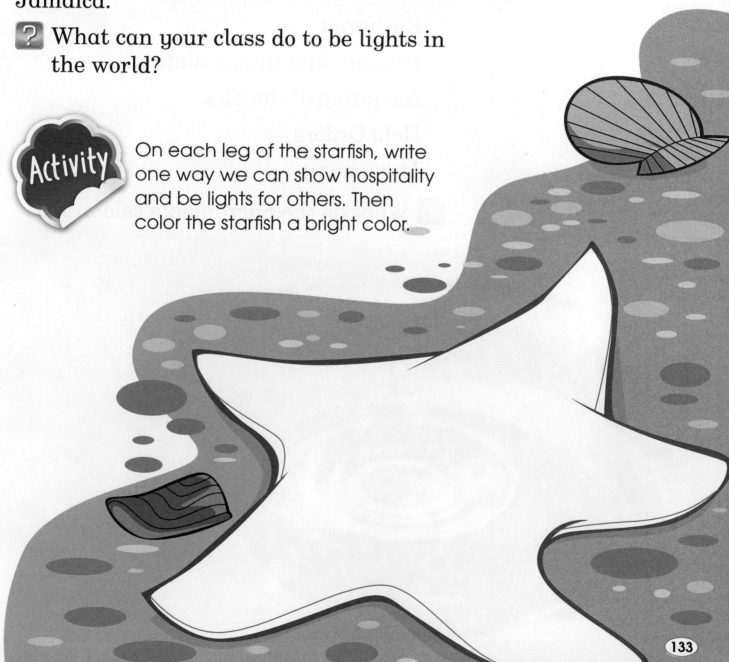

Faith Words
Sacraments
The Sacraments are the seven signs and celebrations of God's love that Jesus gave the Church.

God Is with Us

Jesus gave the Church seven special signs and celebrations of God's love. We call these celebrations the **Sacraments**. The Sacraments celebrate that God is with us. The names of the Seven Sacraments are:

Baptism

Confirmation

Eucharist

Penance and Reconciliation

Anointing of the Sick

Holy Orders

Matrimony

? What do the Sacraments celebrate?

Sharing in God's Love

In the Seven Sacraments, God shares his love and life with us. Each of the Sacraments helps us to grow closer to God.

? How do you think the Sacraments help us grow closer to God?

Catholics Believe

Baptismal Candle

At Baptism, we receive a lighted candle. This reminds us that we are to live as followers of Jesus, who is the Light of the world. We are to be lights in the world.

Activity

Check the boxes next to the Sacraments you have received. Then color the boxes next to the Sacraments you have seen other people receive.

Faith Focus
When do we become
members of the
Church?

Faith Words
Baptism
Baptism is the first
Sacrament that we
celebrate. In Baptism,
we receive the gift
of God's life and
become members of
the Church.

We Celebrate Baptism

Baptism is the first Sacrament that we celebrate. We become a member of the Church.

The priest or deacon pours water on our head or puts us in the water three times. As he does this, he says, "I baptize you in the name of the Father, and of the Son, and of the Holy Spirit. Amen."

The pouring of water and the saying of the words tell us we receive the gift of God's life in Baptism. We receive the gift of the Holy Spirit.

❓ What gifts do we receive at Baptism?

The Gifts at Baptism

In Baptism, Original Sin and any other sins are forgiven. Original Sin is the first sin committed by Adam and Eve. We are born with this sin. When we are baptized, we become members of the Church.

? What happens at Baptism?

Faith-Filled People

Godparents

Godparents help us to grow in faith. They show us how to love God and other people as Jesus taught.

My Baptism

Write your name on the line. Read about what happened at your Baptism.

My name is _____.

I was baptized with

I received the gift of the

I received a lighted

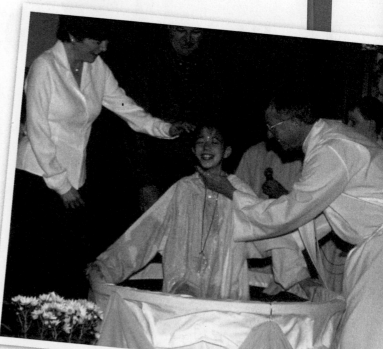

Faith Focus
What do we celebrate
at Confirmation?

Faith Words
▶ **Confirmation**
Confirmation is the
Sacrament in which
the gift of the Holy
Spirit strengthens us
to live our Baptism.

We Celebrate Confirmation

We celebrate **Confirmation** after we
are baptized. Sometimes we celebrate
Confirmation right after Baptism, on
the same day. If we celebrate Baptism
when we are infants, we usually celebrate
Confirmation when we are older.

The bishop, or the priest named by
the bishop, leads the celebration of
Confirmation. During the celebration, he
rubs special oil on the front of our heads.
The oil is called Sacred Chrism. As he
rubs the Chrism, he says, "Be sealed
with the Gift of the Holy Spirit."

The bishop or priest then says, "Peace
be with you." We respond, "And with your
spirit." The Holy Spirit teaches and helps
us to live our Baptism. He helps us live
as followers of Jesus. He
teaches and helps us to be
lights in the world.

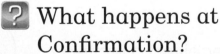 What happens at
Confirmation?

At your Baptism, you became a member of the Church. At Confirmation, the Holy Spirit will give you special help to be a light in the world and welcome others.

I Follow Jesus

Activity

Lights in the World

Draw one way you can be God's light in the world at home, at school, and in your neighborhood.

My Faith Choice

I want to be a light in the world. I will

_____

- -

_____

Pray, "Thank you, Holy Spirit, for helping me to live as a follower of Jesus. Amen."

1. In Baptism, God shares his love and life with us.

2. In Baptism we receive the gift of the Holy Spirit.

3. In Confirmation we are sealed with the gift of the Holy Spirit to help us to live our Baptism.

Chapter Review

Recall

Complete the sentences. Color the O next to the best choice.

1. There are _____ Sacraments.

   O three   O seven

2. _____ gave the Church the Sacraments.

   O Jesus   O The Saints

3. _____ is the first Sacrament that we receive.

   O Eucharist   O Baptism

Write the answer to the sentences below.

4. In Baptism the Church uses

   W _____

5. In Confirmation the Church uses

   O _____

Reflect

How do the Sacraments help us?

_____

_____

Share Share with a partner how you will be a light in the world.

Thank You, Lord

We use water to celebrate the Sacrament of Baptism. Thank God for the gift of water.

Leader   Lord, we thank you for the gift of water.

All   **Thank you, Lord.**

Leader   In Baptism, water is a sign that we are receiving the gift of God's life.

All   **Thank you, Lord.**

Leader   Come and dip your fingers in the water. Pray the Sign of the Cross and remember your Baptism.

All   **Amen!**

With My Family

This Week . . .

In Chapter 10, "Signs of God's Love," your child learned:

▶ Baptism is the first Sacrament we receive.

▶ Through Baptism, God makes us sharers in his life and love. We are reborn as children of God and receive the gift of the Holy Spirit. Original Sin and personal sins are forgiven. We become members of the Church, the Body of Christ.

▶ Confirmation strengthens the graces of Baptism.

▶ Hospitality is welcoming others as children of God. We show that we respect others.

For more about related teachings of the Church, see the *Catechism of the Catholic Church*, 1113–1130 and 1210–1274, and the *United States Catholic Catechism for Adults*, pages 183–197 and 203–209.

■ Sharing God's Word

Read together Matthew 5:14–16. Emphasize that at Baptism, we are joined to Jesus, the Light of the world. Talk about how your family members are living their Baptism and are lights in the world.

■ We Live as Disciples

The Christian home is the first place where children learn to live as disciples. Choose one or more of the following activities to do as a family, or design a similar activity of your own.

▶ Make thank-you cards for godparents. Thank your godparents for helping you grow in faith.

▶ Sign your child on her or his forehead with a small sign of the cross before your child leaves for school. Remind your children that they are to be lights in the world.

■ Our Spiritual Journey

Baptism is the doorway to the Christian life. The ritual of blessing ourselves with holy water reminds us of our Baptism. Integrate the use of this ritual into your daily life. Begin your family prayers by inviting everyone to bless themselves with water while praying the Sign of the Cross.

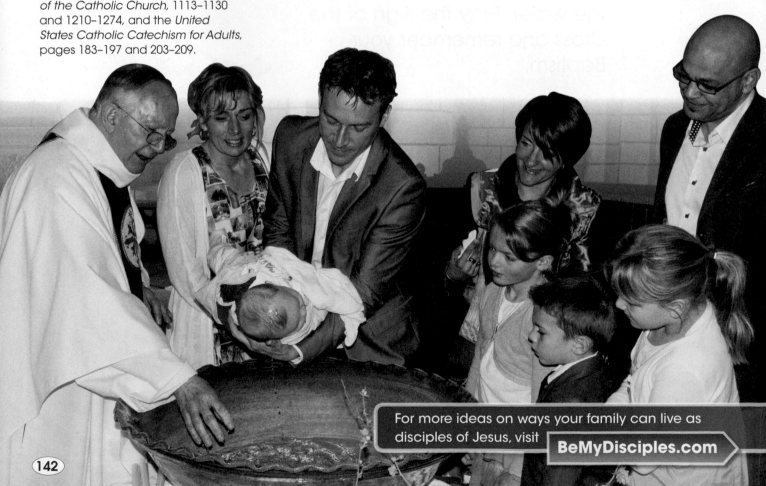

For more ideas on ways your family can live as disciples of Jesus, visit **BeMyDisciples.com**

CHAPTER 11

We Follow Jesus

? What good news have you heard this week?

Followers of Jesus have the best good news to share. Listen to what Jesus tells us about sharing that Good News:

Jesus would soon return to his Father in Heaven. He told his disciples, "Go into the whole world. Tell everyone the good news I shared with you."

BASED ON MARK 16:15

? Who has shared the Good News of Jesus with you?

Disciple Power

Goodness

Goodness is a sign that we are living our Baptism. When we are good to people, we show that we know they are children of God. When we are good to people, we honor God.

Read to Me

Saint Francis of Assisi

Francis sang about the Good News of Jesus. God's love filled his heart.

Everywhere Francis went he told everyone about Jesus. Francis shared with everyone how much God loves them. God loves us so much that he gave us Jesus.

Everything good that Francis saw reminded him of how much God loves us. Today we honor Francis as a Saint.

? What is one way that you and your family tell each other about Jesus?

Singing the Good News

Saint Francis wrote a beautiful song.
It tells about the Good News of God's love.

All the earth 🌑 shouts God's praise.
The sun ☀️ shines out to brighten days.
The moon 🌙 and stars ✨ both shine at night.
The fire 🔥 gives warmth and heat and light.
The wind ☁️ blows strong and gentle.
The rain 🌧 falls making all things new.
Each flower 🌷 and tree 🌳, each bird 🐦 and bee 🐝
And all that live on earth 🌑, in sea 🌊,
Give great praise to God above.
Praise God's goodness.
Praise God's love.

BASED ON THE CANTICLE OF THE SUN

? What good thing in God's creation reminds you of God's love?

Activity

Write one way you can praise God for his goodness.

_____

_____

_____

_____

Faith Focus
Why do we share the Gospel with others?

Faith Words
► **Gospel**
The Gospel is the Good News that Jesus told us about God's love.

The Good News of Jesus

Jesus told everyone the Good News of God's love. Jesus chose followers to help him share this Good News with all people. Disciples share the Good News of Jesus.

Jesus chose Matthew to be one of his first disciples. Matthew was one of the Apostles. Matthew wrote about the Good News of Jesus. He wrote the Good News about Jesus in his **Gospel.** The word *gospel* means "Good News."

? What was the Good News that Matthew wrote about in his Gospel?

Good News of God's Love

The main part of Saint Matthew's Gospel tells about Jesus dying and being raised from the dead. This is the Good News that Saint Matthew wants to share with everyone.

? How do you share the Good News of Jesus?

Catholics Believe

The Four Gospels

Saints Matthew, Mark, Luke, and John each wrote a Gospel about Jesus. The four Gospels are part of the New Testament in the Bible.

 **Activity**

Color the ♡ next to the ways you can share the Good News of God's love.

 Tell people about Jesus.

 Say "Thank you" to someone who is kind to me.

 Make a get-well card for a friend who is sick.

 Be rude to someone who is not kind to me.

Saint Matthew

Tell the Good News

The last story in Matthew's Gospel tells about Jesus returning to his Father in Heaven. In this story, we hear the important work that Jesus gave to his disciples.

Jesus told his disciples, "Go to every land you can. Invite all people to be my disciples. Baptize them in the name of the Father, and of the Son, and of the Holy Spirit. Teach them what I have taught you."

BASED ON MATTHEW 28:19–20

? How do Christians today tell others about the Good News?

Listen to the Good News

The disciples did the important work that Jesus asked them to do. Many people listened to the disciples and the Good News they shared. Many were baptized and became followers of Jesus.

 What do you do to be a follower of Jesus?

 **Activity**

Trace the way to Jesus. Find and circle the things that followers of Jesus share with others.

Faith-Filled People

Blessed Teresa of Calcutta

Mother Teresa was born in a country named Albania. When she was in high school, she knew God was calling her to serve the poorest of the poor. She started the Missionaries of Charity to do that work. Today, the Missionaries of Charity share the Good News of God's love with poor, sick, and dying people around the world.

Love

Peace

Joy

Goodness

Forgiveness

Followers of Jesus Christ

The disciples of Jesus traveled to small villages and to large cities. They walked. They rode donkeys. They traveled in ships.

They did the work that Jesus had given them to do. They told everyone the Good News of Jesus Christ. They baptized people. They taught what Jesus taught them. Many people became followers of Jesus. People called the followers of Jesus *Christians*.

When we hear the Gospel, we come to know Jesus better. We grow in faith. We grow in our love for God and for other people.

? What happens when we hear and listen to the Gospel?

You are a disciple of Jesus. There are many good ways to tell others about Jesus. The Holy Spirit helps you to tell people the Good News about Jesus.

I Follow Jesus

Activity

Tell the Good News

Imagine that you are one of the children in the picture. Write what you want to tell other people about Jesus.

My Faith Choice

Check (√) what you will do this week. I will share what I have written about Jesus with

- ☐ my parents
- ☐ a friend
- ☐ my grandparents
- ☐ someone at church

Pray, "Come, Holy Spirit. Help me share the Good News about Jesus. Amen."

TO HELP YOU REMEMBER

1. The Gospel is the Good News that Jesus told about God's love.

2. Jesus told his disciples to tell everyone the Good News that he shared with them.

3. When we listen to the Gospel, we come to know Jesus better and we grow in faith.

Recall

*Remember the name for Jesus' Good News. Color the spaces with **X**s red. Color the spaces with **Y**s another color.*

Reflect

How does God's love help you? What are the ways you can share God's love with others?

_____

- -

_____

_____

- -

_____

Share | Tell the ways you will share God's love with others to a classmate.

Lord, Help Us to Listen

At Mass, we pray silently before we listen to the Gospel. We trace a small cross on our foreheads, on our lips, and over our hearts. Learn to pray in this new way.

Jesus, be in my thoughts,

on my lips,

and in my heart. Amen.

With My Family

This Week . . .

In Chapter 11, "We Follow Jesus," your child learned:

▶ The Gospel is the Good News about Jesus. Matthew, Mark, Luke, and John are the four Gospel writers.

▶ The last story in Matthew's Gospel is about Jesus telling his disciples to preach the Gospel and to baptize people.

▶ Christians are to treat all people with goodness. Goodness is a Fruit of the Holy Spirit. It is a sign expressing our belief that every person is a child of God. In treating others with goodness, we are cooperating with the graces we received at Baptism.

For more about related teachings of the Church, see the *Catechism of the Catholic Church*, 124–133 and 849–856, and the *United States Catholic Catechism for Adults*, pages 79–85.

▇ Sharing God's Word

Read together Matthew 28:19–20, the story about the commissioning of Jesus' disciples. Or read the adaptation of the story on page 148. Emphasize that Jesus told the disciples to invite all people to be his disciples. Tell how your family shares the Gospel with others.

▇ We Live as Disciples

The Christian home and family is the first place where children learn to live as disciples. Choose one or more of the following activities to do as a family, or design a similar activity of your own.

▶ Saint Francis of Assisi sang about the Good News of Jesus. Invite each family member to share his or her favorite song or hymn that tells about Jesus. Be sure that everyone explains why the song or hymn is his or her favorite.

▶ Invite family members to share one thing that they would like everyone in the family to know about Jesus.

▇ Our Spiritual Journey

When we are good to people, we show we respect them as children of God. We are a sign to them of how much God loves them. We also remind ourselves of our true identity. We grow in respect for ourselves. We are all children of God. Practice the prayer on page 153 with your child. Remind your family that we say this prayer silently when the priest introduces the Gospel at Mass.

For more ideas on ways your family can live as disciples of Jesus, visit **BeMyDisciples.com**

CHAPTER 12

The Catholic Family

? Who belongs to your family?

Like you, Jesus grew up in a family. Listen to what the Bible tells us about Jesus' family.

> When Jesus was a baby, Mary and Joseph presented him to the Lord in the Temple in Jerusalem. When they returned to the family home in Nazareth, Jesus grew up there. He came to know what God wanted him to do.
>
> BASED ON LUKE 2:39–40

? What do these words from the Bible tell you about Jesus' family?

Disciple Power

Fidelity

Fidelity is about keeping our promises. Parents show fidelity when they love and care for their children.

Helping Families

In Landon's family, both parents have jobs. His parents need to work to provide food, clothes, and many other things that a family needs.

Many years ago, not far from Landon's home, the Sisters of the Holy Family started the Holy Family Day Home. It is a place where children stay while both of their parents work.

Landon's parents saw that the Holy Family Day Home was a safe place for Landon to be after school when they were at work. The children learn to respect themselves and others. Landon and the other children play and learn after school.

Holy Family Day Home helps families care for their children. It helps families to grow stronger.

? What do you enjoy doing after school?

Strong Families

Look at this tree. See how big and strong it is. What do you think makes a tree grow to be so strong?

Families can be like trees. They can have strong roots and branches.

The people in a family love and care for each other. They help each other grow strong. There are many people who help a family grow to be strong too.

? Who helps your family grow strong?

 Make a family tree. Draw in the faces of your family members. Write your family name on the tree trunk.

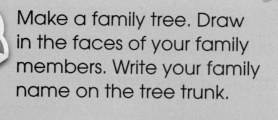

Faith Focus
How do our families help us to grow as children of God?

Faith Words
marriage
A marriage is the lifelong promise of love made by a man and a woman to live as a family.

Matrimony
Matrimony is the Sacrament that Catholics celebrate when they marry.

The Gift of Marriage

When a man and a woman love each other very much, they marry each other. They make a promise to love each other. They promise to live as a family for their whole lives.

The Gospel of John tells us about a **marriage**:

Jesus and Mary, his mother, and the disciples went to a wedding. During the party, the married couple ran out of wine. Jesus blessed six large jars of water, and the water became wine. Everyone was surprised. Everyone was happy. Jesus gave the wine to the married couple.

BASED ON JOHN 2:1–11

? Why do you think Jesus helped the married couple?

Families Are Signs of God's Love

When Catholics get married, they celebrate a special sign of God's love. They celebrate the Sacrament of **Matrimony**. The husband and wife make promises. They promise to always love one another. They promise to honor and respect one another.

A husband and a wife sometimes receive the wonderful gift of children from God. They become parents.

There are many different kinds of families. All families are called to love God and one another. Families are to be signs of God's love in their homes and in the world.

? How does your family share God's love?

Catholics Believe

The Family Church
Our families help us to know and love Jesus. They help us to live as disciples of Jesus. That is why we call our families "the family Church" or "the Church of the home."

Activity

Make a promise that will help your family be a sign of God's love. Share your promise with your family.

Dear Family,
I promise to

_____

- -

_____

- -

_____

so that we can be a sign of God's love in the world.

Faith Focus
How are our families
a sign of God's love?

Families Help One Another

A family is a gift and a blessing from God. Families are a sign of God's love. Christian families are signs of Jesus' love for his followers.

Members of a family share their love with God and with each other. They pray together. They respect each other. They say and do kind things for each other. They take care of each other. They honor and respect each other as children of God.

[?] What are some ways your family members help each other?

Families Love One Another

We learn about God's love in our families. Families pray together. They ask God to help them be loving and kind. Families celebrate the Church seasons together. The members of a family love God and one another.

? What are some ways that you can be part of the Church family?

Saint Elizabeth Ann Seton

Elizabeth Ann Seton is the first person born in America who was named a Saint. Elizabeth and her husband, William, were the parents of five children. They showed God's love to each other and to their children.

Activity

Draw your family as signs of God's love. Show them doing something that helps them grow in God's love. Share your picture with your family.

The Family of God

When we are baptized, we become part of God's family, the Church. Our Church family helps us grow as Catholics.

The Church teaches us about another family called the Holy Family. Mary, Joseph, and Jesus are the Holy Family.

Our family is the Church of the home. Our family helps us to grow in faith. It helps us to live our faith. It teaches us to pray and to care for others as Jesus did.

? What is one way our families teach us about God?

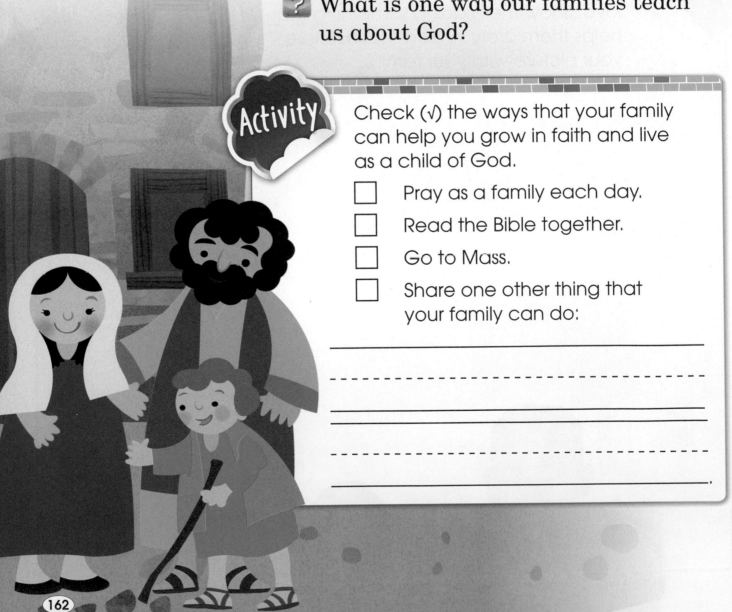

Activity

Check (√) the ways that your family can help you grow in faith and live as a child of God.

☐ Pray as a family each day.

☐ Read the Bible together.

☐ Go to Mass.

☐ Share one other thing that your family can do:

_____

- - - - - - - - - - - - - - - - - - -

_____

- - - - - - - - - - - - - - - - - - -

_____

You are a part of your family. You are also a part of God's family, the Church. God the Holy Spirit helps you to share God's love with the members of your family. When you do this, you honor and respect your parents and the other members of your family.

Activity

Sharing Family Love

Learn to sign these words. Teach the signs to your family. Share God's love with one another.

God   loves

you.

My Faith Choice

This week, I will share God's love with a member of my family. I will sign the message, "God loves you."

Pray, "Thank you, Holy Spirit, for helping me to share God's love with my family. Amen."

1. Christian families are signs of Jesus' love in the world.

2. Members of a family share their love for God with one another.

3. Our families help us to live our faith.

Chapter Review

Recall

Circle the best words to complete each sentence.

1. A _____ is a lifelong promise of love made by a man and a woman to live as a family.

        Baptism   **marriage**

2. _____ is the Sacrament Catholics celebrate when they marry.

        Baptism   **Matrimony**

Read this poem. Fill in the blanks with rhyming words.

Families, families, everywhere _____

show each other love and _____.

They tell us of God's love, you see. _____

God loves each of us, you and _____.

Reflect

What does it mean to honor and respect others?

_____

_____

_____

Share   **Share with your class how you will show honor and respect to your family.**

A Family Blessing

Ask God to bless your family. Pray this prayer now with your classmates.

Leader   Lord God, show your wonderful love to all our families.

Reader 1   Bless our parents and grandparents,

All   **we ask you, Lord.**

Reader 2   Bless our families with life and joy

All   **we ask you, Lord.**

Reader 3   Bless our famllies with the gift of your love.

All   **we ask you, Lord.**

Reader 4   Bless *(say the names silently in your heart)*

All   **we ask you, Lord.**

Leader   Loving Lord, you have made us all. Like a strong tree, you have planted us in the deep love of a family. Help us blossom with respect and honor. Help our family grow in your love,

All   **we ask you, Lord. Amen.**

With My Family

This Week . . .

In Chapter 12, "The Catholic Family," your child learned:

▶ God invites a man and a woman to share their love for him and for one another forever in marriage.

▶ Matrimony is the Sacrament that Catholics celebrate when they marry.

▶ The Christian family is the "Church of the home," or the "family Church."

▶ Families are signs of God's love. Families are the primary place where parents and children experience and grow in faith, hope, and love.

▶ Fidelity helps children and parents grow stronger as a family in their love for God and for one another. Fidelity helps us live the Fourth Commandment.

For more about related teachings of the Church, see the *Catechism of the Catholic Church*, 1601–1658 and 2197–2233, and the *United States Catholic Catechism for Adults*, pages 279–287.

■ Sharing God's Word

Read together Luke 2:41–52, the finding of the twelve-year-old Jesus in the Temple. Emphasize that in the Holy Family, Jesus grew in love for God and for his family. Talk about the things that your family does that help one another grow in love for God and for one another.

■ We Live as Disciples

The Christian home and family is the first place where children learn to live as disciples. Choose one or more of the following activities to do as a family, or design a similar activity of your own.

▶ When we pray as a family, we show that our family loves God. Make an extra effort this week to pray together as a family at least once a day.

▶ Talk about the many ways in which your family is a sign of God's love, for example, when you do kind things for one another, when you pray together, and so on. Encourage one another to continue doing these things.

■ Our Spiritual Journey

A blessing is a sacramental. Sacramentals are sacred signs given to us by the Church. We use blessings to dedicate things or special occasions or people to God. Read and pray the blessing prayer on page 165 together as a family.

For more ideas on ways your family can live as disciples of Jesus, visit **BeMyDisciples.com**

Grandparents and Grandfriends Day

The first grade class was very excited. The children and their teacher were getting ready for Grandparents' Day.

The class was inviting everyone's grandparents to visit for an afternoon. But some children did not have grandparents nearby or still living. What should the class do?

There were elderly people who lived in the parish that did not have family living nearby. The class decided that they would invite some of these people to their Grandparents' Day. They would call them Grandfriends.

WE LIVE IN A COMMUNITY

Each of us is an important member of a family, a parish, a school, and a community. We help each other, and we share our gifts.

Making Connections

No matter how old or how young, we all have something to give. We can help one another. Help the class plan for the Grandparents and Grandfriends Day

with MATH AND SCIENCE

The students and grandparents or grandfriends can make shape art! Use paper and scissors. Cut out shapes, such as triangles, circles, squares, and rectangles. Then, name the shapes and make a design using all of the shapes. Glue it on a large piece of paper.

with CREATIVE ARTS

Draw two cartoons. Have one cartoon show an older person teaching a younger person. Have the other cartoon show you teaching your grandparent or a grandfriend something. You can learn from each other!

with LANGUAGE ARTS

The class will send invitations to the grandparents and grandfriends asking them to come to their class. Create an invitation that the class can use.

Faith Action

We work together to help each other.
Write one way you help your family.

_____

- -

_____

Unit 3 Review

A. Choose the Best Word

Complete the sentences. Color the circle next to the best choice.

1. Advent, Christmas, Lent and _____ are all seasons of the Church year.

   ◯ winter   ◯ Easter

2. Jesus gave the Church seven _____ to help us grow closer to God.

   ◯ Commandments   ◯ Sacraments

3. The first _____ of Jesus told everyone the Good News of God's love.

   ◯ family   ◯ disciples

4. When we listen to the _____, we come to know Jesus better and grow in faith.

   ◯ Gospel   ◯ music

5. Christian families are _____ of Jesus' love for his followers.

   ◯ signs   ◯ homes

B. Show What You Know

Use purple, green, or gold to color the circle next to each season or time of the Church year. Use the correct color for each season or time.

◯ Advent   ◯ Ordinary Time

◯ Easter   ◯ Christmas

◯ Lent

C. Connect with Scripture

What was your favorite story about Jesus in this unit? Draw something that happened in the story. Tell your class about it.

D. Be a Disciple

1. *What Saint or holy person did you enjoy hearing about in this unit? Write the name here. Tell your class what this person did to follow Jesus.*

_____

- - - - - - - - - - - - - - - - - - - -

_____

2. *What can you do to be a good disciple of Jesus?*

_____

- - - - - - - - - - - - - - - - - - - -

_____

_____

- - - - - - - - - - - - - - - - - - - -

_____

A Time to Celebrate

Once Jesus invited a man named Levi to follow him. Levi said, "Yes!" He was so happy that he gave a big party. But some people did not like Levi. They said to Jesus' disciples, "We are so mad! Jesus is at a party with sinners. That is very bad!"

But Jesus said, "Of course I am here with sinful people. I am here to forgive them and give them peace. When sinful people stop doing what is wrong and turn their hearts to God, it is the best time to celebrate."

BASED ON LUKE 5:27–32

What I Know

What is something you already know about these faith words?

Prayer

_____

- -

_____

Mass

_____

- -

_____

Put an X next to the faith words you know.
Put a ? next to the faith words you need to learn more about.

____ patience   ____ Galilee   ____ wisdom

____ Eucharist   ____ miracle   ____ peace

A Question I Have

What question would you like to ask about the Mass?

_____

- -

_____

- -

_____

CHAPTER 13

We Pray

? What are some of your favorite prayers?

Sometimes we pray for ourselves. At other times we pray for our family and friends. Jesus taught his followers how to pray. Listen to what Jesus said.

You do not need to use many words when you talk to God. Talk to God from your heart. BASED ON MATTHEW 6:7

? What are some prayers you pray with your Church family?

Disciple Power

Patience

We act with patience when we listen carefully to others. We pay attention when they are helping us.

The Church Follows **Jesus**

Prayer Partners

The sixth graders at Nativity parish wanted to help the first graders. They considered being lunch buddies or reading friends. Finally, they chose to be their prayer partners.

The sixth graders sat with their prayer partners when they went to church. They helped the first graders to learn the words to the prayers. They helped the first graders to sing the hymns. They taught them when to stand and when to sit and when to kneel.

Just as Jesus taught his disciples to pray, the sixth graders helped the first graders learn how to pray.

❓ Who helps you learn how to pray?

Prayer Partner Promises

Make a prayer partner promise with someone at home or in class. Read the promises below. After you sign your promise, ask your prayer partner to sign a promise, too.

My Promise

_____

- -

My prayer partner is _____.

I promise to

- Choose a time and place to pray.

- Get help to talk and listen to God each day.

- Pray with my partner.

_____

- -

Signed: _____

Prayer Partner Promise

_____

- -

I promise to be a prayer partner for _____.

I promise to

- Help my partner find a time and place to pray.

- Help my partner to talk and listen to God each day.

- Pray with my partner.

_____

- -

Signed: _____

God Hears Our Prayers

Friends and family members listen and talk to each other. Talking and listening are ways of sharing. We can share what is on our minds and in our hearts.

Prayer is listening and talking to God. It is sharing with God what is on our minds and in our hearts.

We can pray anywhere and anytime. The Holy Spirit helps us to pray. When we pray, we grow in our love for God.

❓ When do you pray? What is your favorite way of praying?

Activity

Prayers to God

Discover some different ways to pray.

You can pray to God. There are many ways. You can offer God your joy in a prayer of praise. I praise you, God for

_____

- -

_____.

Another way to pray that is very fine indeed, is to ask our giving God for all the things you need. I ask you, God for

_____

- -

_____.

When you need forgiveness for something you have done, you can say, "I'm sorry, God, for hurting anyone." I'm sorry, God, for

_____

- -

_____.

Think of all the many gifts with which you have been blessed. Remember, then, to say, "Thanks, God. You are the very best!" Thank you, God, for

_____

- -

_____.

Catholics Believe

Meal Prayers

We pray before and after meals. We ask God to bless us and the food we eat. We ask God to help people who do not have enough food.

Jesus Shows Us How to Pray

Jesus prayed all during his life. Talking and listening to God his Father was a very important part of his life.

Sometimes Jesus prayed alone. Jesus told us that it is important for us to pray alone, too.

When you want to pray, go to your room to be by yourself. Talk and listen to God your Father. God will hear you and will answer your prayer.

BASED ON MATTHEW 6:6

Sometimes Jesus also prayed with his family. Sometimes Jesus prayed with his friends. Sometimes Jesus prayed with his neighbors.

? What did Jesus tell us about prayer?

Thank you, God, for loving me. Bless my family and friends. Amen.

We Pray

Like Jesus, we can pray anywhere and anytime. Sometimes we pray alone. Sometimes we pray with others. We pray with our family. We pray with our friends. We pray with our Church family.

? Where is your favorite place to pray? Why is it your favorite place?

Activity

Draw your favorite place to pray.

Faith-Filled People

Saint Thérèse of the Child Jesus

Thérèse of the Child Jesus (of Lisieux) is also called the Little Flower. Thérèse found a favorite place to pray. When she was young, she would pray in the space between her bed and the wall. The Church celebrates the feast day of Saint Thérèse of the Child Jesus on October 1.

God Always Listens

Jesus told us that God is our Father. God the Father always wants us to talk with him in prayer. He wants us to share with him what is on our minds and in our hearts.

We do what Jesus taught us. We tell God the Father we love him. We thank him for his blessings.

We ask God to take care of our families and us. We ask God to help other people. We ask God to forgive us and to help us to live as his children.

? Why do we pray?

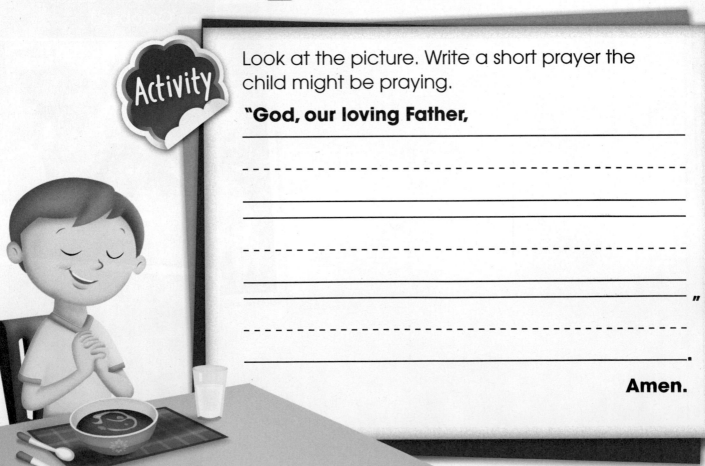

Activity

Look at the picture. Write a short prayer the child might be praying.

"God, our loving Father,

_____

- - - - - - - - - - - - - - - - - - - -

_____

_____

- - - - - - - - - - - - - - - - - - - -

_____

_____ **"**

- - - - - - - - - - - - - - - - - - - -

_____ **.**

Amen.

The Holy Spirit teaches us to pray. We can talk to God about anything. We can pray anywhere and anytime. Patience helps us to pray. It helps us to spend time with God.

I Follow Jesus

Activity

Times to Pray

Fill in the chart. Name something or someone you can pray for at different times during the day.

Morning	
Afternoon	
Evening	

My Faith Choice

This week, I will pray to be a patient person. I will pray in the morning, afternoon, and evening.

Pray, "Thank you, Holy Spirit, for helping me be patient with others. Amen."

1. Prayer is listening and talking to God.

2. When we pray, we grow in our love for God.

3. God always listens to our prayers.

Chapter Review

Recall

Color the ◯ if the sentence is true.

Color the ☐ if the sentence is false or not true.

T **F**

1. We can talk to God about anything. ◯ ☐
2. We can talk to God anywhere. ◯ ☐
3. We can pray only by ourselves. ◯ ☐
4. Jesus prayed often. ◯ ☐
5. God cannot hear our prayers. ◯ ☐

Reflect

What prayers do you like to pray?

_____

- -

_____

- -

_____

- -

_____

Share   **Share with a partner when you like to pray and why.**

Hail Mary

We pray to Mary, the Mother of Jesus. She teaches us to pray. Learn these words from the Hail Mary. Pray them often. Pray them alone and with your family.

Leader   Mary, the Mother of Jesus, loves us. Let us lift up our hearts in prayer to her.

All   **Hail, Mary, full of grace, the Lord is with thee. Blessed art thou among women, and blessed is the fruit of thy womb, Jesus.**

Leader   Mary taught her Son Jesus how to pray. Let us ask Mary to teach us as well.

All   **Holy Mary, Mother of God, teach us how to pray. Since Jesus was your little boy, you surely know the way. Amen.**

With My Family

This Week . . .

In Chapter 13, "We Pray," your child learned:

► Prayer is simply listening and talking to God.

► Jesus is our example for how we are to pray.

► We can pray anywhere and anytime. We can share with God everything and anything that is on our minds and in our hearts.

► We demonstrate patience when we listen carefully to people and pay attention when they are helping us. Patience helps us to spend time with God in prayer even when we want to do something else.

For more about related teachings of the Church, see the *Catechism of the Catholic Church*, 2558–2619, and the *United States Catholic Catechism for Adults*, pages 466–468 and 476–477.

■ Sharing God's Word

Read together Matthew 7:7–11. Emphasize that prayer is listening and talking to God. We can pray anywhere and anytime. God knows what we need before we ask him.

■ We Live as Disciples

The Christian home and family is a school of discipleship. It is the first place where children learn to live as disciples of Jesus. Choose one of the following activities to do as a family, or design a similar activity of your own.

► Go for a walk together. Thank God for everything you see and hear.

► Family prayer time helps us be aware that God is always with us. Evaluate your family prayer time. Do what it takes to integrate time for prayer into your family's daily activities and schedule.

■ Our Spiritual Journey

Mary is the first disciple of her son, Jesus. She is the model of what it means to be a disciple of Jesus. Devotion to Mary is central to the life of Catholics. Incorporate frequent conversation with Mary into your prayer time. Seek direction for your life by meditating on the mysteries of the Rosary.

For more ideas on ways your family can live as disciples of Jesus, visit **BeMyDisciples.com**

CHAPTER 14

We Are Peacemakers

? Who has forgiven you?
Whom have you forgiven?

Forgiving others shows our love for one another. Christians forgive one another. Jesus tells us to forgive people who have hurt us. Jesus said,

"Ask God to forgive your sins and to help you forgive those who have hurt you."

BASED ON MATTHEW 6:12

? What did Jesus teach about forgiveness?

Peace

We live as peacemakers when we forgive those who have hurt us. We ask for forgiveness when we have hurt others. These actions bring peace to us and to others.

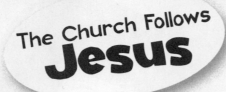

The Church Follows **Jesus**

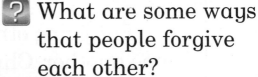

Read to Me

The Pope Makes Peace

Saint John Paul II was riding in the back of his car. He was greeting and waving to people.

A man came out of the crowd and shot the Pope. The Pope was hurt but soon got better.

Pope John Paul II went to the prison and visited the man who shot him. He put his arms around the man and forgave him. The Pope made peace with the man who had hurt him. He showed us what Jesus wants us to do.

? What are some ways that people forgive each other?

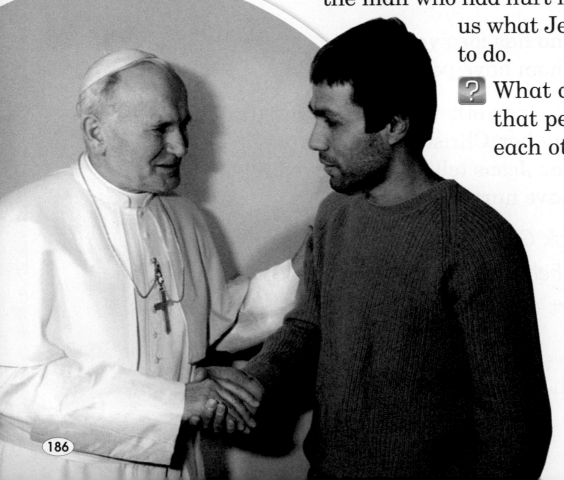

Acting as Peacemakers

Jesus said,

*"Blessed are the peacemakers,
for they will be called children of God."*

MATTHEW 5:9

When Saint John Paul II forgave the man who shot him, he was acting as a peacemaker. Jesus wants us to act as peacemakers, too.

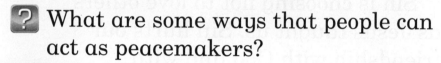 **?** What are some ways that people can act as peacemakers?

 **Activity**

Draw a picture of yourself acting as a peacemaker.

Faith Focus
How does sin hurt God, ourselves and others?

Faith Words
sin
Sin is choosing to do or say something that we know is against God's Laws.

Making Peace

We can use words and actions to help others. At other times, we can choose to use our words and actions to hurt others. When we do, we are not obeying God. We **sin.**

Sin is choosing to do or say something that we know is against God's Laws. When we sin, we turn away from God's love.

Sin is choosing not to love others as Jesus taught us. Sin hurts our friendship with God and with other people.

? What happens when we sin?

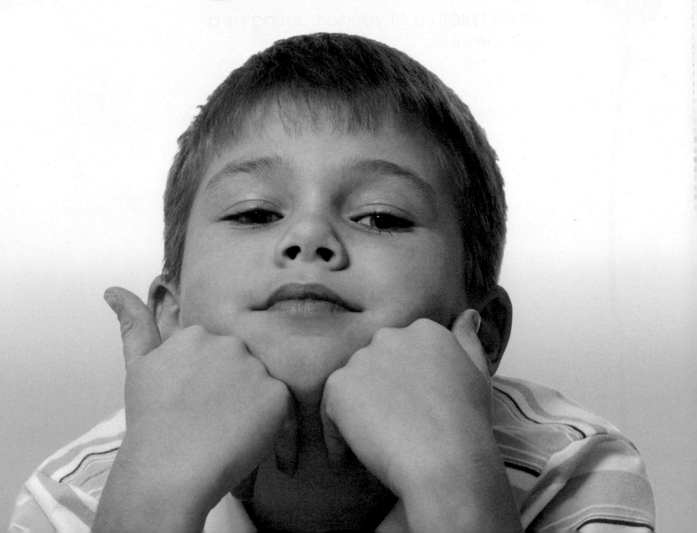

Making Good Choices

Sometimes we choose to do what is right. Sometimes we choose to do what is wrong. We pray to the Holy Spirit to help us make a good choice.

 Who helps you to make good choices?

Catholics Believe

Sign of Peace

Each Sunday at Mass, we shake hands or share another sign of peace with one another. This shows that we want to forgive those who have hurt us. We want to live together as one family of God.

Activity

Look at these pictures. Pretend you are making a movie. With a partner, act out a picture showing a good choice.

Faith Focus
Why is it important to say "I am sorry" when we choose to do or say something that is wrong?

Asking for Forgiveness

When we choose what is right, we are showing our love for God and others. When we choose what is wrong, we need to say we are sorry. Saying we are sorry is a sign of love.

We feel sorry when we sin. We want to be forgiven. We want to make up for our sin.

We need to say that we are sorry to the people whom we hurt by our sin. We need to ask for forgiveness. We want everything to be right again.

We also need to say that we are sorry to God when we sin. We tell God that we are sorry. We ask for forgiveness because we love God. God will always forgive us because he loves us.

? Why do we ask for forgiveness when we sin?

Words!

Words can hurt, or words can heal. Words can show that we are sorry. Words can show that we want forgiveness, and for everything to be right again.

? What words can you use if you hurt someone?

Activity

Circle the words that show you are sorry. Also circle the words that show you forgive someone.

Faith-Filled People

Saint John Vianney

Father John Vianney was a priest. He helped people who were sorry for their sins. Railroad tracks were built to his town because so many people wanted to come to him to receive forgiveness for their sins. The Church celebrates the feast day of Saint John Vianney on August 4.

I'm sorry.

Let's be friends.

I don't like you.

It's my fault.

It's O.K.

Go away.

Forgiving Others

Jesus tells us to forgive people who have hurt us. He tells us to forgive them over and over again.

One day, Jesus' disciple, Peter, asked Jesus, "How many times do I have to forgive someone who hurts me? Seven times and then stop?"

Jesus looked at Peter and said, "No, not seven times. You must learn to forgive over and over again."

BASED ON MATTHEW 18:21–22

Sometimes it is not easy to do what Jesus wants us to do. Sometimes we do not feel like forgiving people who have hurt us. The Holy Spirit helps us forgives others.

We open our hearts with love when we forgive others. We show our love for God and for one another. We are peacemakers.

? How do you show forgiveness? How do other people show you forgiveness?

The Holy Spirit teaches you and helps you to forgive others. He also helps you to ask for forgiveness. When you forgive someone, you are a peacemaker.

Activity

A Forgiving Tree

In the leaves, write words or draw actions that show forgiveness.

My Faith Choice

This week, I will use the forgiving words or actions that I wrote or drew in the activity. I will bring peace to others.

Pray, "Thank you, Holy Spirit, for teaching and helping me to live as a peacemaker. Amen."

1. Sin hurts our friendship with God and others.

2. When we say that we are sorry, we show that we love God and others.

3. When we say that we are sorry, we ask for forgiveness from others and from God.

Chapter Review

Recall

Choose the best word and write it in the space for each sentence.

forgive	peace	sin

1. When we _____ we turn away from God's love.

2. Jesus asks us to _____ others.

3. We bring _____ when we show our love for others.

Reflect

How will you choose to be a peacemaker?

_____

_____

_____

_____

Share   Tell a partner how you can act as a peacemaker.

Prayer of Mercy

At the beginning of Mass, we ask God for his mercy. The word mercy reminds us that forgiveness is a gift of God's love. Pray this prayer together.

Leader Let us bow our heads and think a moment about ways we have chosen what was wrong and failed to love God and others. *(Pause.)*

For the times we have hurt others, Lord, have mercy.

All **Lord, have mercy.**

Leader For the times we have not told the truth, Christ, have mercy.

All **Christ, have mercy.**

Leader For the times we have refused to say, "I am sorry" or "I forgive you," Lord, have mercy.

All **Lord, have mercy.**

Leader Have mercy, loving God. Have mercy on us. Help us to forgive and to be forgiving. Help us live as peacemakers.

All **Amen.**

With My Family

This Week . . .

In Chapter 14, "We Are Peacemakers," your child learned:

▶ People make choices to help others or to hurt others. We can choose to follow or reject God's Laws.

▶ People can sin. Sin always hurts our relationship with God and with others. When we sin, we need to say that we are sorry both to God and to those whom we have hurt. We need to ask for forgiveness. We need to reconcile our relationships with God and with people.

▶ We live as peacemakers when we are honest in our relationships and with God. When we forgive others, we are peacemakers.

For more about related teachings of the Church, see the *Catechism of the Catholic Church*, 1420–1484 and 1846–1869, and the *United States Catholic Catechism for Adults*, pages 235–236.

■ Sharing God's Word

Read together Matthew 18:21–35, the parable of the Unforgiving Servant. Emphasize that Jesus teaches us that we are to forgive others over and over again, as God always forgives us when we are truly sorry for our sins.

■ We Live as Disciples

The Christian home and family is a school of discipleship. Choose one of the following activities to do as a family, or design a similar activity of your own.

▶ When you participate in Mass this week, pay close attention to the prayer of mercy that we pray at the beginning of Mass. Remember that the word *mercy* reminds us that God's forgiveness is a gift of his love.

▶ Name ways that people show that they are sorry. Talk about ways that members of your family can both show forgiveness to one another and accept forgiveness from one another.

■ Our Spiritual Journey

In this chapter, your child prayed a prayer of mercy. This is one of the three forms of prayer that the Church uses for the Penitential Act in the Introductory Rites of the Mass. Through this prayer, we are reconciled with God and one another. We enter into the celebration of the Eucharist in right relationship with God and one another, as peacemakers. Read and pray together the prayer on page 195.

For more ideas on ways your family can live as disciples of Jesus, visit **BeMyDisciples.com**

CHAPTER 15

We Go to Mass

❓ When do you say thank you to others?

We can thank people in many ways. Our Church thanks God in a special way at Mass. Listen to what the Bible tells us about giving thanks to God.

> It is good to give thanks to the LORD,
> to sing praise to your name, Most High.
>
> PSALMS 92:2

❓ When do you say thank you to God?

Perseverance

Perseverance helps us to live our faith when it is difficult. We do not give up even when it is not easy to do something good.

The Church Follows **Jesus**

Read to Me

Sharing God's Love

First Holy Communion was a special day for Peyton and the other children of Saint Mary's Church. At the end of Mass, they heard Father Julio say, "Go in peace, glorifying the Lord by your life."

At the next religion class, Peyton asked Mrs. Hensle, "What did Father Julio tell us to do? I don't understand."

Mrs. Hensle explained, "Father Julio said we need to show we are children of God by what we say and do." The children talked about what they could do.

They visited elderly people living in a retirement home. They played a board game together. This was their way of saying thank you for the gift of First Holy Communion. They shared God's love with other people.

❓ How can you share God's love with people?

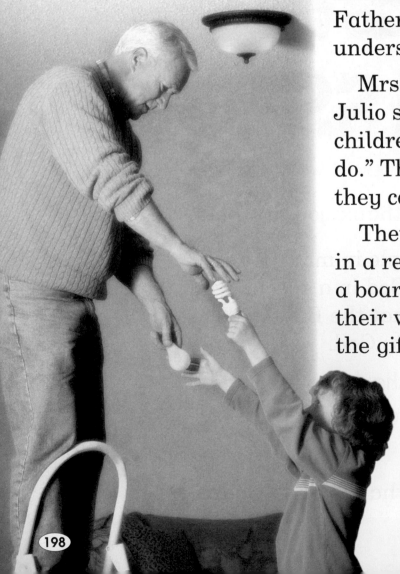

Loving God and Others

Read the sentences below. Put the number of the sentence next to the word that shows you are sharing God's love.

☐ help   ☐ share   ☐ listen

1 Dad, I see you are raking the leaves.

May I _____?

2 If you are feeling sad and

need to talk to someone, I will

_____.

3 Are you hungry? I can _____

my lunch with you.

Faith Focus
Why does our Church family gather to celebrate Mass?

Faith Words
▶ **Mass**
The Mass is the most important celebration of the Church.

We Gather at Mass

The **Mass** is the most important celebration of the Church. We gather as the People of God. We give glory to God. We show that we love and honor God

We gather as people who believe in Jesus and want to live as his followers. We gather to worship God.

We often begin the Mass by singing a hymn. Our singing helps us to remember we are part of a community. We are part of the family of God.

❓ What do you see and hear at Mass?

We Sing Glory to God

Together, we pray the Sign of the Cross. This reminds us of our Baptism. We remember that we belong to Jesus and are members of the Church.

Together, we honor God. We sing or say a beautiful prayer called the Gloria. We sing the words the angels sang at Jesus' birth: "Glory to God in the highest!"

? How does the Sign of the Cross remind us of our Baptism?

Catholics Believe

Peacemakers

At the end of Mass we are told, "Go in peace." Peacemakers share God's love with people Jesus taught that God blesses peacemakers. Jesus said, "Blessed are the peacemakers, for they will be called children of God" (Matthew 5:9).

Activity

Draw you and your family at Mass.

We Listen to God's Word

We listen to readings from the Bible at every Mass. God tells us about his love for us. On Sunday we listen to three readings. After the first two readings, we give thanks and say, "Thanks be to God."

Then we stand. The priest or deacon proclaims the Good News of the Gospel. We honor God as we say, "Praise to you, Lord Jesus Christ."

The priest or deacon helps us to understand God's Word. We come to know and love God. We learn ways to live as Jesus taught.

We tell God that we have listened to his Word. We pray the creed. We stand and say, "I believe." We tell God we believe in him.

Then we pray for other people and for ourselves. We trust that God hears us.

❓ Why do the readings at Mass help us?

Activity

Praise God!

Loving God,

I listen to your Word at Mass. Your Word makes me want to give you thanks and praise. Your Word invites me to believe and pray.

I want to thank you for

_____

- -

_____ .

I want to praise you for

_____

- -

_____ .

I want to be a disciple of Jesus by

_____

- -

_____ .

Thank you, God for listening to my words.

Your child,

_____

- -

_____

P. S. I love you!

Faith-Filled People

Priests

Priests are the bishop's coworkers. They lead us in the celebration of the Mass. They teach us what Jesus taught. They help us to live as followers of Jesus.

Faith Focus
What do we do when we celebrate the Eucharist?

Faith Words
Eucharist
The Eucharist is the Sacrament in which we receive the Body and Blood of Christ.

We Give Thanks to God

At Mass we celebrate the **Eucharist.** The Eucharist is the Sacrament in which we receive the Body and Blood of Christ. The word *eucharist* means "to give thanks."

In the celebration of the Eucharist, we give thanks to God. We remember and do what Jesus did at the Last Supper. The Last Supper is the meal that Jesus ate with his disciples on the night before he died.

At the Last Supper Jesus took bread and said, "This is my body." Then he took the cup of wine and said, "This is my blood."

BASED ON MATTHEW 26:26–28

At Mass, the priest repeats the words and actions of Jesus. We receive the Body and Blood of Christ in Holy Communion.

? What do we do at Mass that Jesus did at the Last Supper?

At Mass, you can listen to God's Word. You learn ways to live as a follower of Jesus. In the celebration of the Eucharist, you give thanks to God. You can try to pay attention at Mass, even when it is hard.

I Follow **Jesus**

Activity

To Do at Mass

Check (√) the things you can do at Mass.

- ☐ Pay attention.
- ☐ Listen to the readings.
- ☐ Pray aloud with my church family.
- ☐ Sing songs to praise God.
- ☐ Say a thank-you prayer to God.

My Faith Choice

This week, I will show my love for God and others. I will

_____

_____ .

_____

_____ .

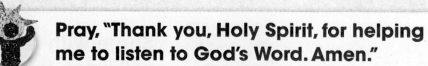
Pray, "Thank you, Holy Spirit, for helping me to listen to God's Word. Amen."

TO HELP YOU REMEMBER

1. At Mass we worship God.

2. At Mass, we listen to readings from the Bible.

3. At Mass, we celebrate and share the Eucharist.

Chapter Review

Recall

Draw a line to match the words on the left with their meanings.

Words	Meanings
Last Supper	The celebration in which we listen to the Word of God. We say thank you to God.
Mass	The Sacrament in which we receive the Body and Blood of Christ.
Eucharist	The meal Jesus ate with his disciples on the night before he died.

Number the following sentences in the order they happen at Mass.

☐ We celebrate Eucharist and receive Holy Communion.

☐ We listen to the Word of God.

☐ We gather together to worship God.

Reflect

What do we do at Mass?

_____

- -

_____

Share   **Share with a classmate how you will listen to the Word of God.**

Thank You, God

We can pray quietly in our hearts and we can pray aloud.

Leader Think about God's Word to us in the Bible. *(Pause.)* For the gift of your holy Word, we say,

All **Thank you, God.**

Leader Let us all remember Jesus. Think about Jesus. *(Pause.)* For the gift of your Son, Jesus, we say,

All **Thank you, God.**

Leader Think about people who share God's love with you. *(Pause.)* For the gift of the people who are your Church, we say,

All **Thank you, God.**

Leader Think about the Mass. *(Pause.)* For the gift of the Body and Blood of Christ, we say,

All **Thank you, God. Amen.**

With My Family

This Week . . .

In Chapter 15, "We Go to Mass," your child learned:

▶ The Mass is the most important celebration of the Church.

▶ During the Liturgy of the Word, we listen to the readings from the Bible.

▶ In the Liturgy of the Eucharist, we remember and do what Jesus did at the Last Supper. The bread and wine become the Body and Blood of Jesus.

▶ We receive the Body and Blood of Christ in Holy Communion.

For more about related teachings of the Church, see the *Catechism of the Catholic Church*, 1322–1405, and the *United States Catholic Catechism for Adults*, pages 215–227.

■ Sharing God's Word

Read together Matthew 26:26–29, the account of the Last Supper. Or read the brief adaptation of the story on page 204. Emphasize that at Mass the bread and wine become the Body and Blood of Christ. Discuss the importance of participating in Mass.

■ We Live as Disciples

The Christian home and family is a school of discipleship. Choose one of the following activities to do as a family, or design a similar activity of your own.

▶ At the end of Mass, we are dismissed with these or similar words: "Go in peace, glorifying the Lord by your life." Choose one thing your family can do together to serve and glorify the Lord this week.

▶ Your child has learned that perseverance means that we try our best even when it is hard. Discuss times that this might be hard to do and that the Holy Spirit will help.

■ Our Spiritual Journey

The psalms are prayers that represent the array of faith experiences. They are both personal and communal. They heighten our memory of God's loving plan for creation and Salvation. Choose and memorize a variety of verses from the psalms. Pause throughout the day to pray them. Pray them at times of joy, sadness, lament and thanksgiving.

For more ideas on ways your family can live as disciples of Jesus, visit **BeMyDisciples.com**

CHAPTER 16

Jesus Shows God's Love

? Which foods are your family's favorites?

Healthy foods help us to grow. Jesus shared food with many people. At the Last Supper, Jesus said to his disciples,

"This is my body, which will be given for you; do this in memory of me."

LUKE 22:19

? How do these words from the Bible remind you of the Mass?

The Church Follows **Jesus**

Read to Me

Wisdom

Wisdom helps us to know what God wants us to do. It helps us to make the right choices to live a holy life.

CRS Rice Bowl

The Bible has many stories of Jesus sharing meals with people. Like Jesus, we can share food with people too.

Each year during Lent, many Catholics participate in CRS Rice Bowl. Catholics put a small box on the table where they eat. Each family member puts money in the box.

At the end of Lent, Catholic families bring the box with the money to church. All the boxes are collected.

The money is used to buy food and clean drinking water for people who need them. When we help people in need, we are sharing God's love too.

[?] What is one way that you can share God's love with people?

CRS CATHOLIC RELIEF SERVICES **RICE BOWL**

Activity

Gifts to Share

People who participate in CRS Rice Bowl give gifts of money to share with people in need. You can share your gifts with people around you.

- Sit in a circle with your classmates.

- Write your name at the top of the list shown on this page.

- Pass your book to the person sitting on your left.

- Write something nice about the person whose book you have. Write it next to the grains of rice.

- Then pass that book to the left.

- Keep writing and passing books until the lists are filled.

Now look at the list. See how many gifts you have! Choose one gift from your list that you can share with others. Then add it to this prayer.

All: Loving God, thank you for giving me gifts to share.

Each Person: Thank you for my gift of

_____

- -

_____.

I will share it with others.

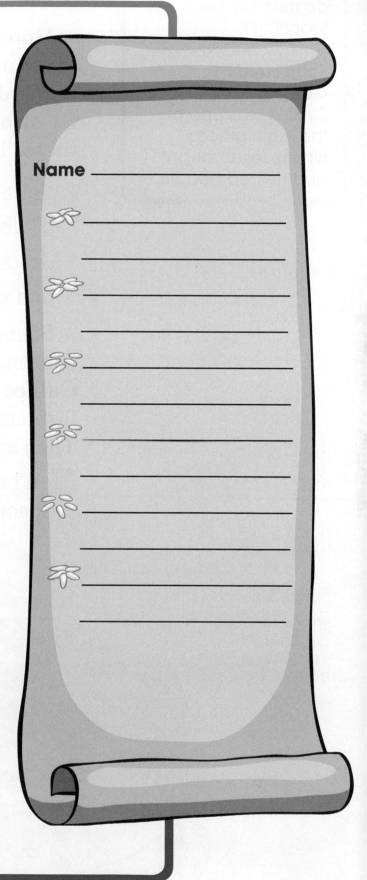

Name _____

Faith Words
► **Galilee**
Galilee was one of
the main places
where Jesus taught
and helped people.

Jesus Shares God's Love

Many of the first disciples of Jesus lived in **Galilee.** Galilee was the place where Jesus did much of his teaching. He also helped many people who lived there. The Gospel of Mark tells us,

Jesus came to Galilee to tell the people all about the Good News of God's love. Jesus said, "Turn your hearts to God and accept his love." BASED ON MARK 1:14–15

Some people in Galilee were fishermen. They fished in the Sea of Galilee for their food. Other people were farmers. They grew fruit and barley. They made bread from the barley.

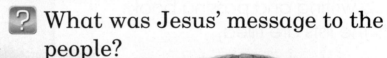 What was Jesus' message to the people?

Jesus Helps People

Jesus traveled all over Galilee sharing God's love and helping people. He cured sick people. He forgave sins. He cared for people.

People began to follow Jesus everywhere he went. The Gospel of Mark tells us,

People were amazed at Jesus. They praised God and said, "We have never seen anyone like him before!"

BASED ON MARK 2:12

? What are the ways we can praise God?

Catholics Believe

Grace

The word *grace* means "gift." Grace is the gift of God's life and love. Grace helps us to share God's love with people. It helps to us to live as children of God.

Activity

Find the names on the map. Write the words in the right places in the sentences.

- Jesus was born in

  _____

  -

  _____.

- Jesus lived in

  _____

  -

  _____.

- Jesus ate fish from the Sea of

  _____

  -

  _____.

Find these places on the map. Circle the words on the map.

Sea of Galilee

Nazareth

Bethlehem

Jesus Feeds the People

One time, Jesus was teaching near the Sea of Galilee. A very large crowd of people gathered to hear Jesus. This is what happened.

It became late and the people were hungry. But Jesus' followers had only five loaves of bread and two fish. Jesus took the bread and the fish and prayed. He blessed the food. His followers gave the food to the people. Everyone ate until they were full.

BASED ON MATTHEW 14: 15–16, 19–20

? What did Jesus share with the people?

Jesus Shares God's Love

Jesus fed the people not just because they were hungry for food. He knew they were also hungry for God's love. Jesus taught the people about God's love.

? What was one way that Jesus shared God's love with the people?

Activity

Feeding the Hungry

Read each sentence about the story of Jesus feeding the people. Number the sentences in the order that they happened in the story.

_____ People ate until they were full.

_____ A large crowd of people followed Jesus.

_____ Jesus blessed the food.

_____ There were only five loaves of bread and two fish.

In the basket, draw or write what you would do with the leftover food.

Faith-Filled People

Saint María de Jesús

Sister María dedicated her life to serving the poor and sick in Mexico. She loved going to Mass. Receiving Holy Communion helped her to treat people as Jesus did. On May 21, 2000, Pope John Paul II named Sister María de Jesus Mexico's first woman Saint.

Faith Focus
What is one way to share God's love?

Faith Words
▶ **miracle**
A miracle is something only God can do. It is a sign of God's love.

Jesus Cares for People

The story of Jesus sharing the **bread** and fish tells about a **miracle**. A miracle is something only God can do. It is a special sign of God's love.

The story of Jesus feeding the people shows how Jesus shared God's love with the people. Jesus took care of the people.

Jesus asks us to take care of one another. This is one way we share God's love with people.

? What do you do to share God's love with other people?

The Holy Spirit helps you to show God's love and care for others. The Holy Spirit's gift of wisdom helps us to make choices for living a holy life. When you share God's love, you are living a holy life.

I Follow Jesus

Activity

Sharing God's Love

In the space, write about or draw yourself sharing God's love with others.

My Faith Choice

I will share God's love with my family. I will

_____

- -

_____ .

Pray, "Thank you, Jesus, for teaching me how to share God's love. Amen."

1. Jesus saw that the people were hungry and gave them all enough to eat.

2. Jesus showed people that God cares for them.

3. Jesus teaches us to care for people.

Chapter Review

Recall

Draw a line to connect the words in Column A with their meanings in Column B.

Column A

1. Galilee

2. bread and fish

3. grace

4. miracle

5. wisdom

Column B

food Jesus gave the people

helps us to live a holy life

gift of God's love

a sign of God's love

where Jesus taught

Reflect

What did Jesus do to show people that God cares for them?

_____

_____

_____

_____

_____

Share Tell a classmate how you show people that God loves them.

A Blessing Prayer

Blessing prayers tell God we know that all good things come from him. Pray this blessing prayer together.

Leader   Father, you give us life.

All   **Blessed be God.**

Leader   Father, you care for everyone.

All   **Blessed be God.**

Leader   Jesus, you came to fill us with God's love.

All   **Blessed be God.**

Leader   Jesus, you showed us how to care for people.

All   **Blessed be God.**

Leader   Holy Spirit, you fill us with grace.

All   **Blessed be God.**

Leader   Holy Spirit, you help us to care for others.

All   **Blessed be God.
Amen.**

With My Family

This Week . . .

In Chapter 16, "Jesus Shares God's Love," your child learned:

- Jesus fed a large crowd with only five loaves of bread and two fish (Matthew 14:15-20).

- This story tells that Jesus took care of people to remind them of God's love for them.

- This story is one of the miracle stories in the Gospels and reveals God's loving care for people and all creation.

- Wisdom is a Gift of the Holy Spirit. It helps us to know God's will for us and to make good choices.

For more about related teachings of the Church, see the *Catechism of the Catholic Church,* 302–308 and 547–550, and the *United States Catholic Catechism for Adults,* pages 79–80, 215–216, and 222–223.

■ Sharing God's Word

Read together Matthew 14:15-20, the account of Jesus feeding the crowd. Or read the adaptation of the story on page 214. Emphasize that everyone ate until they were full. Discuss that this is a sign of God's caring love for all people.

■ We Live as Disciples

The Christian home and family is a school of discipleship. Choose one of the following activities to do as a family, or design a similar activity of your own.

- Jesus fed the hungry people to show them that God loves and cares for them. Choose to do one thing this week to show people that God loves and cares for them.

- When you go grocery shopping this week, purchase food to donate to the local food pantry. Join with others to be a sign of God's loving care for all people.

■ Our Spiritual Journey

A blessing prayer is an expression of God's generosity and love. Our lives can be blessing prayers. The best way to bless God is to share our material and spiritual blessings with others, especially people in need. Pray the blessing prayer on page 219 together as a family.

For more ideas on ways your family can live as disciples of Jesus, visit **BeMyDisciples.com**

Good Foods. Good Choices.

Miss Grant, a first grade teacher, eats carrot sticks instead of potato chips at lunchtime. One day Miss Grant decided her class needed to think about eating healthful foods. She asked the class, "What will happen if I fill up my car's gas tank with water instead of gasoline? Will my car work?"

"No," said Celia. "It will ruin your car," added John.

"Yes," Miss Grant agreed. "Sometimes we fill our bodies up with food and drinks that are not good for us. Let's talk about what we can eat and drink to take good care of our bodies."

WE TREAT ALL LIFE AS GOD'S GIFT TO US

Every child is a gift from God. God wants us to love and respect ourselves. We love and respect others too.

Making Connections

God has given us the gift of life. He wants us to take care of ourselves. One way we take care of ourselves is by eating healthful foods and by exercising.

with MATH AND SCIENCE

You are learning about the basic food groups. Each of the food groups tells us about foods we can eat to take care of our bodies. Write or draw your favorite foods in each of the food groups. Tell a partner why eating these foods are good for our bodies.

with CREATIVE ARTS

Act out a television commercial about showing respect for our bodies. Tell why it is important to exercise and eat healthful foods.

with LANGUAGE ARTS

Look at a picture or list of foods from each of the food groups. Make a list of the healthy snack foods. Share the list with your class and family. Take care of yourself and eat healthy!

Faith Action

Show God you want to take care of yourself. Write a healthy food you will eat this week.

_____

- -

_____ .

Unit 4 Review

A. Choose the Best Word

Complete the sentences. Color the circle next to the best choice.

1. Every Sunday, the people of the Church gather to celebrate _____.

   ○ Confirmation   ○ Mass

2. At the _____, Jesus said, "This is my body" and "This is my blood."

   ○ Last Supper   ○ First Easter

3. Prayer is listening and talking to _____.

   ○ our parents   ○ God

4. We need to ask for _____ when we have hurt someone.

   ○ forgiveness   ○ punishment

5. Jesus fed a crowd with two fish and _____ loaves of bread.

   ○ two   ○ five

B. Show What You Know

Circle the number next to your favorite prayer. Tell your class when you can pray it.

1. Sign of the Cross   4. Hail Mary

2. Our Father   5. Grace Before Meals

3. Glory Be

C. Connect with Scripture

What was your favorite story about Jesus in this unit? Draw something that happened in the story. Tell your class about it.

D. Be a Disciple

1. *What Saint or holy person did you enjoy hearing about in this unit? Write the name here. Tell your class what this person did to follow Jesus.*

_____

- -

_____

2. *What can you do to be a good disciple of Jesus?*

_____

- -

_____

_____

- -

_____

The Way to Heaven

One day a young man asked Jesus, "What must I do to live forever with God in heaven?" Jesus said, "Keep God's commandments."

The young man said, "I have always kept them." "Wonderful!" Jesus said. "Now sell all your things, give to the poor, and follow me."

The young man turned away. He did not want to give away his things. Jesus felt sad. "If a person loves their things more than they love God, it will be hard to get to heaven."

BASED ON MARK 19:16–23

What I Know

What is something you already know about these faith words?

Christians

_____

- -

_____

Ten Commandments

_____

- -

_____

Put an X next to the faith words you know. Put a ? next to the faith words you need to learn more about.

_____ Great Commandment	_____ respect	_____ community
_____ worship	_____ honor	_____ patron Saints

A Question I Have

What question would you like to ask about the Ten Commandments?

_____

- -

_____

_____

- -

_____

CHAPTER 17

The First Christians

? What are some things that make you and your family smile?

The first followers of Jesus were like a family. Listen to what the Bible tells us about Jesus' followers:

> The disciples were filled with joy and the holy Spirit.

ACTS 13:52

? What do these words from the Bible tell you about Jesus' followers?

Understanding

God the Holy Spirit gives us the Gift of Understanding. Stories in the Bible help us understand God's love for us. Stories in the Bible help us understand what Jesus taught us.

The Church Follows **Jesus**

Saint Martin de Porres

Read to Me

Martin de Porres loved God. He became a religious brother. The Holy Spirit helped Brother Martin to live as a disciple of Jesus. Brother Martin served people with a joyful heart.

Brother Martin lived in South America. He worked with poor people. He opened a home for children whose parents had died or could not care for them. He opened a hospital and schools. He also took care of animals that were sick or hungry.

The Church named Brother Martin a Saint. Today many people follow the good example of Saint Martin de Porres.

❓ Who is someone you know who helps people as Saint Martin de Porres did?

Joyful! Joyful!

The Bible tells us to be joyful like Saint Martin.

Shout with joy to the LORD.

BASED ON PSALM 98:4

Jesus himself wants us to be people filled with joy. Jesus said,

"If you do what I have taught and follow me, you will remain in my love. . . . I have told you this so that my joy may be in you and your joy may be great."

BASED ON JOHN 15:10–11

? **What are the ways that you are joyful?**

A Joyful Heart

Draw yourself in the heart. Then sing from the heart and make a joyful noise together.

If you're joyful and you know it
    when you pray,

If you're joyful and you know it
    when you play,

If you're joyful and you know it,
    then your happy heart will show it
    by the way you follow Jesus every day.

Christians Share Stories

Families like to hear stories and tell stories. The people of our Church like to hear and tell stories too. They have told and listened to stories from the beginning of the Church.

The Church tells stories that help us understand God's love for us. The Church tells stories about Jesus. These stories help us to know what it means to be a Christian. **Christians** are followers of Jesus Christ. They believe in Jesus. Christians are baptized and live as Jesus taught us.

❓ Who are Christians?

Following Jesus

The first Christians followed Jesus. We follow Jesus today. We listen to the stories about Jesus at Mass, at school, and from our families. Our church, school, and families help us live as followers of Jesus.

? How does your school help you follow Jesus?

Faith-Filled People

Saint Paul the Apostle

Paul became an Apostle after Jesus' Resurrection. Paul traveled by land and by sea to teach people about Jesus. He invited them to believe in Jesus. The Church celebrates the feast day of Saint Paul the Apostle on June 29.

Activity

Following Jesus

On each of the road signs, write or draw one way that followers of Jesus act today.

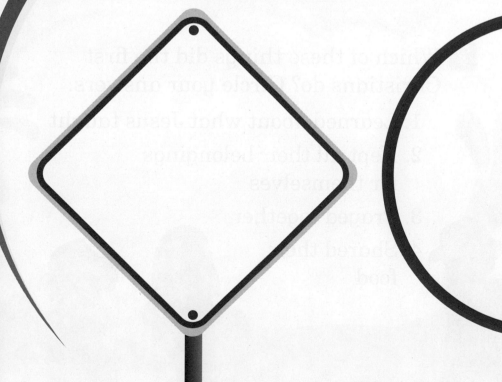

Christians Love One Another

Our Church shares stories about what Christians did a long time ago. We can read these stories about the first Christians in the New Testament.

The first Christians spent time learning what Jesus taught. They shared their money and belongings with one another. They prayed together. They shared bread together. They praised God together.

Many people saw how the first Christians treated one another with kindness and love. Soon many other people became followers of Jesus.

BASED ON ACTS OF THE APOSTLES 2:42, 45–47

? Which of these things did the first Christians do? Circle your answers.

1. Learned about what Jesus taught
2. Kept all their belongings for themselves
3. Prayed together
4. Shared their food

The First Christians

This story tells us how the first Christians lived. It is a story that has been shared from the very beginning of the Church.

? What other stories do you know about Jesus or the first Christians?

Activity

Living as a Christian

Think of a follower of Jesus you know. Check one thing that this person does. Act it out for your class.

Person I Know

- ☐ Prays with others
- ☐ Cares for others
- ☐ Tells me about Jesus
- ☐ Shares with me

Catholics Believe

Patron Saints

The Saints help us remember how to love as Jesus taught. The Church names some Saints to be patron Saints. Patron Saints help us live as followers of Jesus in a certain way. Saint Martin de Porres is the patron Saint of African Americans and health-care workers.

We Live as Jesus Taught

The first Christians did what Jesus did. They did what Jesus taught. Jesus taught us to love God and to love one another.

The stories about the first Christians teach us how to live as children of God. The first Christians showed their love for God. They prayed and shared the Eucharist. They thanked God for everything.

The first Christians showed their love for one another. They shared what they had with each another. They helped people in need.

? How can we live like the first Christians?

Each day you try your best to live as Jesus taught. The Holy Spirit helps you to understand how Jesus wants you to treat people. You treat people with kindness. This brings people joy. It also fills your heart with joy.

I Follow Jesus

Activity

Write a √ mark in the box next to each thing that you can do this week to live as Jesus taught.

☐ Say my prayers.

☐ Hurt someone.

☐ Learn about Jesus.

☐ Share my toys.

☐ Obey my parents.

☐ Play fairly.

☐ Speak unkind words.

☐ Help at home.

☐ Pay attention at school.

☐ Be a litter-bug.

My Faith Choice

This week, I will do one of the Christian acts that I have checked. I will

_____

_ _

_____.

 Pray, "Thank you, Holy Spirit, for helping me to act as Christians do. Amen."

1. Christians believe in Jesus Christ and do what he taught.

2. The first Christians gathered together and loved God and one another.

3. Christians today show their love for one another just as the first Christians did.

Chapter Review

Recall

*Read each sentence. Circle **Yes** if the sentence is true. Circle **No** if it is not true.*

1. The first Christians shared stories about Jesus.

Yes   **No**

2. The first Christians prayed together.

Yes   **No**

3. The first Christians shared their belongings with one another.

Yes   **No**

Complete the sentence using the words in the word box.

Jesus	love	people

_____

- -

I _____ God and

_____

- -

I love _____

_____

- -

as _____ taught.

Reflect

How do you live as a joyful follower of Jesus?

Share | **Share with your class ways we can live as joyful followers of Jesus.**

Praise the Lord

A sign of peace shows that we want to live as Jesus taught. We share a sign of peace at Mass.

Leader   Listen to these words from Saint Paul's letter to the first Christians.

Reader   Always be joyful. Never stop praying. Always give thanks. This is what God wants you to do in Jesus Christ.

BASED ON 1 THESSALONIANS 5:16–18

The word of the Lord.

All   **Thanks be to God.**

Leader   We are God's joyful people, and so we pray: Praise the Lord, for he is good!

All   **Praise the Lord, for he is good!**

Leader   We thank you, Lord, for the Church.

All   **Praise the Lord, for he is good!**

Leader   Let us now share a sign of peace with one another.

All   *(Share a handshake or other sign of peace and friendship.)*

With My Family

This Week . . .

In Chapter 17, "The First Christians," your child learned:

▶ The first Christians gathered to express their faith and belief in Jesus.

▶ The first Christians listened to the teachings of the Apostles. They shared all that they had with one another, especially with people in need. They gathered to pray and break bread, or share the Eucharist.

▶ Christians today do the same things that the first Christians did. Every member of the Church is called to cooperate with the grace of the Holy Spirit and work together to live as Jesus taught.

▶ The Holy Spirit helps us to understand ways to live as followers of Jesus.

For more about related teachings of the Church, see the *Catechism of the Catholic Church,* 849–852, 1397, and 2030–2046, and the *United States Catholic Catechism for Adults,* pages 118–119.

◼ Sharing God's Word

Read together the Acts of the Apostles 1:42–47 together, an account of the life of the first Christians. Or read the adaptation of the story on pages 232–233. Emphasize that the first Christians shared their possessions with people in need and were known for their love for one another.

◼ We Live as Disciples

The Christian home and family is a school of discipleship. Choose one of the following activities to do as a family, or design a similar activity of your own.

▶ Identify ways that your family lives as the first Christians did. Talk about ways you pray, learn about Jesus, and share things as a family. Invite each family member to choose one thing that they can do to help your family live as a Christian family.

▶ Decide on one way in which your family can share your time and possessions with other people in your parish, school, or neighborhood. For example, write get-well cards to those who are sick or homebound.

◼ Our Spiritual Journey

The peace that comes from living in communion with God, others, and all of creation is the ultimate destination of our spiritual journeys. You have received the Gift of Understanding to help you achieve that peace. Pray the prayer on page 237 at mealtime and include a sign of peace.

For more ideas on ways your family can live as disciples of Jesus, visit **BeMyDisciples.com**

CHAPTER 18

We Love God

 **What are some good rules for a family?**

God's rules are called Commandments. Listen to what the Bible tells us about them:

God said, "I will show love to those who love me and keep my commandments."

BASED ON EXODUS 20:6

 **What is one of God's rules that you know?**

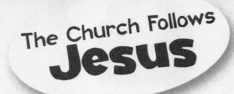
Disciple Power

Knowledge

The gift of Knowledge helps you to know and to follow God's rules. It also helps you to know things that are against God's rules and to not do them.

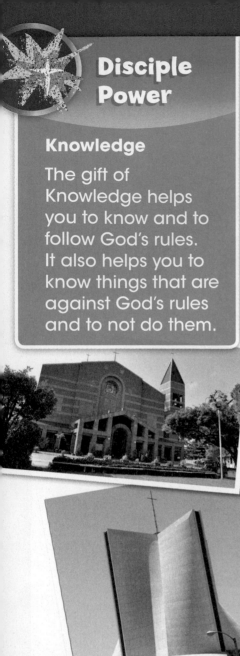

Building Churches

God has given us ten important rules called the Ten Commandments. Catholics follow the Ten Commandments. The First Commandment tells us to keep God first in our lives. Here is a story of how Father Richard followed the First Commandment

Father Richard studied art before he became a priest. He also worked as an engineer. After he became a priest, Father Richard used his gifts to live the First Commandment. He helped build new churches and repair old churches.

Catholics gather in churches to worship God. Our churches show that we love God above all else.

? How do the people of your church help you to keep God first in your life?

My Catholic Church

Many people belong to the Catholic Church. Baptism makes them members of the Church. Each week the people who belong to the Catholic Church gather to celebrate the Eucharist together. The Eucharist makes us one family.

? What are the ways that you help your church family?

My Church

Write the names of some people you know who belong to the Catholic Church.

_____

- -

_____

_____

- -

_____

Write the name of your Catholic family, your parish.

_____

- -

_____

Imagine you are an engineer like Father Richard. A nearby town needs a new church. Tell a partner what this new church could look like.

Faith Focus
Why did God give us the Ten Commandments?

Faith Words
► **Ten Commandments**
The Ten Commandments are the laws that God has given us to help us to live as children of God.

God's Commandments

In Crazy Town, all the rules are  **STOP** means **go**, and *FAST* means **s – l – o – w.** When people say *yes*, they really mean *no*.

The meow,

and the bark.

You turn **OFF** the

when it gets .

The 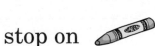 are all stuck in the .

If you pass a 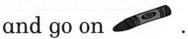 , you really .

 stop on

and go on .

You put on , then crawl into .

So, to keep your

from becoming a ,

you had better stay out of Crazy Town.

 What kinds of rules are there in Crazy Town? Why do you think it would be hard or easy to live in Crazy Town?

Moooo!

RED

242

The Ten Commandments

We have rules at home, at school, and in our community. Good rules helps us to live together in peace.

The Bible tells us that God gave us ten very special rules. These rules are the **Ten Commandments**. He gave us the Ten Commandments because he loves us. The Commandments are the laws that God has given us help us to live as children of God.

The Ten Commandments tell us how we are to love God and other people. They tell us to care for ourselves and for all creation.

❓ Why are the Ten Commandments important?

Catholics Believe

Cathedrals

There are many kinds of churches. The cathedral is the bishop's church. The name of the Pope's cathedral is Saint John Lateran.

Activity

With your classmates, act out one way you can show your love for God. Act out one way you can show your love for your family.

Jesus Teaches Us

Jesus taught us that the Ten Commandments are important. He said,

"All of the Ten Commandments are important. A person who obeys the commandments and teaches other people the commandments will be called greatest in heaven."

BASED ON MATTHEW 5:18–19

Jesus taught us that we are to live the Ten Commandments. Jesus showed us how to love God. Jesus prayed to his Father. He always did what God the Father asked him to do.

❓ What did Jesus teach us about the Ten Commandments?

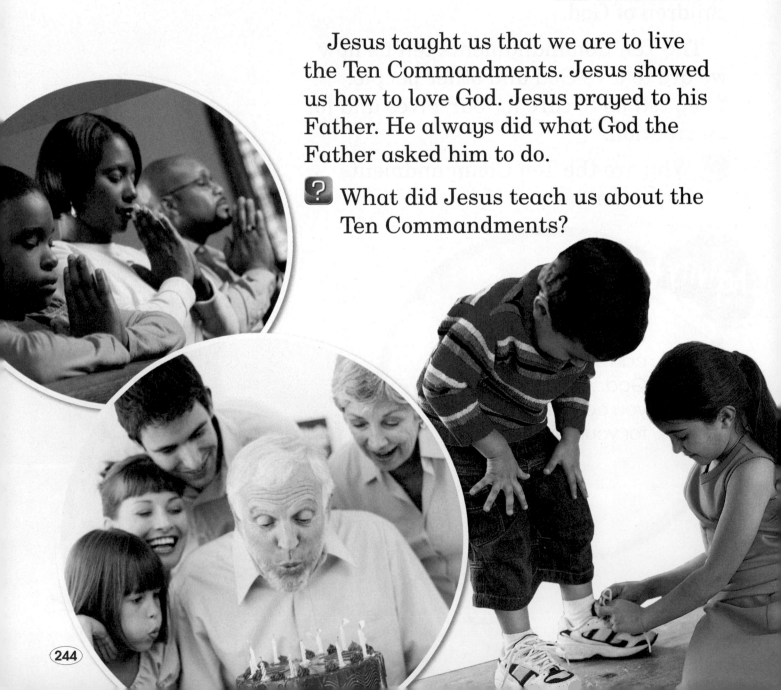

Love One Another

Jesus showed us how to love one another. He was kind to everyone. Jesus told us to treat people as he did. He said,

"I give you a new commandment: love one another. As I have loved you, so you also should love one another."

John 13:34

We are to live the Ten Commandments. We are to treat people as Jesus taught us to do.

? How are the people in the pictures showing their love for God? How are they showing their love for people?

Faith-Filled People

Saint Clare and Saint Agnes

Clare of Assisi and Agnes of Assisi were sisters. They gave up everything to show their love for God. Saint Clare's feast day is August 11. Saint Agnes's feast day is November 16.

Activity

Thank God for all that he has done for you. Use words and pictures to make a thank-you card.

Thank You, God, for...

Faith Focus
What did Jesus teach about the first three Commandments?

Faith Words
worship
We worship God when we love and honor God more than anyone and anything else.

We Love God

The First, Second, and Third Commandments tell us ways to show our love for God.

The First Commandment tells us that we are to **worship** only God. We love God more than anything and anyone else.

The Second Commandment tells us to honor God. We speak God's name with love and respect.

The Third Commandment tells us to keep Sunday as a holy day. Every Sunday, we gather with our church family for Mass. We give thanks and praise to God for all that he has done for us.

❓ How do we worship God?

You are learning about the Ten Commandments. Your family and the Church will help you. The Holy Spirit will always help you to know the Ten Commandments and to live them. The Holy Spirit's gift of knowledge helps you to worship and honor God.

I Follow Jesus

Activity

A Letter to God

Write a letter. Tell God how you will show your love for him this week.

Dear God,

_____

- -

_____

_____

_____

_____

- -

_____.

My Faith Choice

Read the letter you wrote to God. Write one way you will show your love for God this week.

_____

- -

_____.

Pray, "Thank you, Holy Spirit, for helping me to show my love for you. Amen."

1. The Ten Commandments teach us to worship God.

2. The Ten Commandments teach us to speak God's name with love and respect.

3. The Ten Commandments teach us to take part in Mass on Sundays.

Chapter Review

Recall

Draw lines to match the words in Column A with their meanings in Column B.

Column A

1. First Commandment

2. Second Commandment

3. Third Commandment

Column B

a. Keep Sunday holy.

b. Worship only God.

c. Speak God's name with respect.

Complete each sentence using the words in the box.

Mass	Sunday

Catholics gather every _____.
to worship God.

We worship God at _____.

Reflect

How do the Ten Commandments help us?

_____

_____

_____

Share Share one way you live the First, Second, and Third Commandments.

An Act of Love

When we pray an act of love, we tell God that we love him with all our heart. Pray these words at home with your family. Pray them now with your class.

Group 1 O my God, you created me. You share your love with me. You are all good.

All **I love you, God, with my whole heart.**

Group 2 O my God, you gave me your Commandments. You want me to live well. You want me to live as your child.

All **I love you, God, with my whole heart.**

Group 3 O my God, you gave me Jesus to teach me how to love, and to show me how to treat people as he did.

All **I love you, God, with my whole heart. Amen.**

With My Family

This Week . . .

In Chapter 18, "We Love God," your child learned:

▶ God gave us the Ten Commandments.

▶ The Ten Commandments tell us ways to live as children of God.

▶ The First, Second, and Third Commandments tell us to love, honor, and worship God above all else.

▶ Jesus taught us to live the Ten Commandments. We are to love God and people as Jesus taught.

▶ Knowledge is one of the seven Gifts of the Holy Spirit. It helps us to know how we are to live and to follow God's will.

For more about related teachings of the Church, see the *Catechism of the Catholic Church*, 2052–2195, and *the United States Catholic Catechism for Adults*, pages 341–369.

◼ Sharing God's Word

Read together John 13:34–35 about Jesus giving his disciples the New Commandment. Or you can read an adaptation of the story on page 245. Emphasize that by his example, Jesus showed us how to love God and one another. He showed us how to live the Ten Commandments.

◼ We Live as Disciples

The Christian home and family is a school of discipleship. Choose one of the following activities to do as a family, or design a similar activity of your own.

▶ Attend Mass together as a family on Sundays. Plan an activity for after Mass that the family can enjoy together.

▶ When you gather for dinner this week, invite family members to share one thing that they did that day to show their love for God. Then give thanks and praise to God.

◼ Our Spiritual Journey

Knowing your way as you journey though life is vital. Knowing where you want to go and how to get there is essential. We can never reach our ultimate goal alone. Pray the prayer on page 249 with your family to help keep your priorities in life in the right order.

For more ideas on ways your family can live as disciples of Jesus, visit **BeMyDisciples.com**

CHAPTER 19

We Love Others

? What are some of the ways that you show your love for your family?

Listen to what the Bible tells us about God's Commandments:

God gave us the commandments. He gave us the commandments so that we may live as friends with him and other people.

BASED ON DEUTERONOMY 6:20-25

? What do the Commandments help us do?

Temperance

Having more things does not make us happy. Temperance helps us to know the difference between what we need and what we just want to have. It is important to know what will really make us happy.

Helping People in Need

Read to Me

Our parish helps us live as friends with God and one another. It helps us to live the Ten Commandments.

Some parishes have a group called the St. Vincent de Paul Society. This group helps people in need. Families give them things they do not really need. The group gives these things to people who do need them.

The group helps people to visit doctors and dentists. They run camps in the summertime for children. The St. Vincent de Paul Society shows people how much God loves them.

? What are some of the ways that you see people being kind to one another?

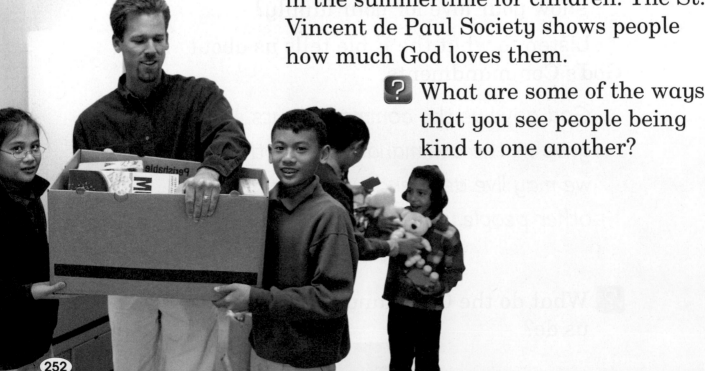

Kindness and Love

You can be like the people in the St. Vincent de Paul Society. You can show respect and love for people. You can care for others. You can act with kindness.

❓ **What is one way you show that you care for others?**

Activity

Circle the words that show ways to act with kindness and love.

```
b  l  a  u  s  e  r  v  e  y
c  m  t  w  h  e  e  l  o  l
s  c  a  r  e  u  g  x  o  v
r  y  s  h  a  r  e  b  p  l
f  o  r  g  i  v  e  l  n  h
```

Write one way you can act with kindness and love today.

_____

- -

_____

_____

- -

_____

Faith Focus
What do the Ten
Commandments
teach about respect?

Faith Words
respect
We show people
respect when we love
them because they
are children of God.

honor
We honor people
when we treat them
with great respect.

We Respect People

The first three Commandments tell us to show our love for God. The rest of the Ten Commandments tell us that we are to **respect** other people and ourselves.

We show respect when we treat and **honor** other people and ourselves as children of God. Showing respect is a way to show kindness and love.

We show respect to people in many ways. We listen carefully to one another. We are polite and kind. We are fair to one another.

We also show respect to ourselves in many ways. We take care of our bodies. We act safely.

❓ What do the rest of the Ten Commandments teach us?

Activity

A Handful of Respect

The Ten Commandments help you show respect for others and yourself.

- Trace the dotted lines to make a hand.

- On the palm, write your name.

- On each finger, write a way you can show respect for someone.

- On the thumb, write a way you can respect yourself.

Faith-Filled People

Saint Vincent de Paul

Vincent de Paul showed us how to live the Ten Commandments. He treated all people with respect. He cared for people who were lonely. The Church celebrates the feast day of Saint Vincent de Paul on September 27.

Faith Focus
How are we to treat
things that belong to
someone else?

We Care for Things

The Ten Commandments tell us to respect what belongs to us. They teach us that we are to respect what belongs to other people, too. We are to take good care of the things that we have.

We show respect for what belongs to others. We are to ask before we borrow their things. We are to return the things that we borrow. We do not steal.

The Ten Commandments also teach us that we are to share our things with others.

? What is one way that you can care for and share with others?

Honor and Respect

As children in God's family, we care for and respect the gifts God gives us. We care for and respect what belongs to us and others. When we do this, we honor and show our love for God.

? What are some of the gifts that God gives us to care for?

Catholics Believe

Collection at Mass

At Mass on Sunday there is a collection. The collection takes place at the beginning of the Liturgy of the Eucharist. The people of the parish share their money to help the Church.

Activity

Look at the pictures. What could the children say to show care and respect?

_____

- -

_____

LET'S TAKE A SHORTCUT THROUGH THE FLOWERS.

LOOK AT MY FLOWERS. WHAT HAPPENED?

We Tell the Truth

The Ten Commandments teach us that we are to be honest. We are honest when we tell the truth. We are not being honest when we lie.

It is important to tell the truth. When we tell the truth, we show respect for ourselves and other people. Lying shows that we do not respect ourselves and other people.

Jesus himself told us to tell the truth. He said,

"Always tell the truth. Say yes when yes is the truth. Say no when no is the truth."

BASED ON MATTHEW 5:37

We are followers of Jesus. We show our love and respect for him when we live and speak the truth. When we tell the truth, people trust us.

❓ Why is it important to be honest and tell the truth?

When you are kind and fair, you treat people with respect. You love people as Jesus taught. When you tell the truth, you are a disciple of Jesus.

I Follow Jesus

Activity

Fill in the blanks in the story.

I ask a friend, "May I please borrow your markers?

_____

- -

I will take good _____

of them." When I am finished, I will return the markers

"_____ "

- -

and say, _____ .

My Faith Choice

Check (✓) ways you will show respect for other people. I will

☐ tell the truth.   ☐ share my things.

☐ say kind words.   ☐ play safely.

 Pray, "Thank you, God, for teaching me to show respect for other people. Amen."

1. We are to treat ourselves and others as children of God.

2. We are to show respect for other people.

3. We are to tell the truth.

Chapter Review

Recall

*Read each sentence. Circle **Yes** if the sentence is true. Circle **No** if it is not true.*

1. Respecting others is a way to show love.

   Yes   **No**

2. Listening to one another shows respect.

   Yes   **No**

3. Taking care of what belongs to others shows respect.

   Yes   **No**

4. Telling lies shows respect.

   Yes   **No**

5. Sharing our things shows respect.

   Yes   **No**

Reflect

What is one way you will act as a child of God?

_____

- -

_____

- -

_____

Share   **Share with your class why it is important to act as children of God.**

Lord, Hear Our Prayer

We pray for one another. Pray together:

Leader   God, you love us. For people who are hungry, we pray,

All   **Lord, hear our prayer.**

Leader   For people who need a home, we pray,

All   **Lord, hear our prayer.**

Leader   For people who are sick, we pray,

All   **Lord, hear our prayer.**

Leader   For people who are sad or lonely, we pray,

All   **Lord, hear our prayer.**

Leader   Everyone pray quietly for someone. *(Pause.)* We pray,

All   **Lord, hear our prayer. Amen.**

With My Family

This Week . . .

In Chapter 19, "We Love Others," your child learned:

▶ The Fourth through Tenth Commandments tell us to love and respect other people, ourselves, and all of God's creation.

▶ The last seven of the Ten Commandments name the ways that we are to live the second part of the Great Commandment and truly live as children of God.

▶ Temperance is a virtue that helps us to know the difference between what we need and what we simply want to have.

For more about related teachings of the Church, see the *Catechism of the Catholic Church*, 2052–2074 and 2196-2557, and the *United States Catholic Catechism for Adults*, pages 375–455.

■ Sharing God's Word

Read together Acts of the Apostles 2:42–47. Emphasize that this story tells about the first Christians living the Commandments as Jesus taught. Name the things that the first Christians did to show how they lived the Ten Commandments.

■ We Live as Disciples

The Christian home and family is a school of discipleship. Choose one of the following activities to do as a family, or design a similar activity of your own.

▶ Read together a children's book about treating people with respect. Discuss why showing respect is at the heart of our love for others.

▶ Have each family member create two lists of their possessions. On one list, write things that you really need. On the second list, write things you like but do not truly need. Choose items you might give away to a charitable group.

■ Our Spiritual Journey

We are a pilgrim people. We make our earthly journey together. In this chapter, your child prayed for others. This is called a prayer of intercession. Intercessory prayer is a prayer that we offer on the behalf of others. Read and pray together the prayer on page 261.

For more ideas on ways your family can live as disciples of Jesus, visit **BeMyDisciples.com**

CHAPTER 20

We Live as a Community

? Who do you know in your neighborhood?

Jesus taught us how to live together.

Jesus said, "Love God with all your heart, with all your soul, and with all your mind. This is the first and greatest commandment. The second is like this one: Love others as much as you love yourself." BASED ON MATTHEW 22:34–39

? How do good neighbors and friends treat each other?

Disciple Power

Justice

We practice justice when we treat people fairly. People who are just live as Jesus taught.

Saint Peter Claver

Father Peter Claver did what Jesus had taught. He helped people who were being treated unjustly. The people had been taken from their homes in Africa. They were put on ships that went far away. They were going to be sold as slaves.

The guards tried to stop Father Peter from going on the ships, but he would not be stopped. God gave him strength. Father Peter was a very brave man.

The ships were hot and dirty. The people had no water to drink or to wash with. Many of them were very sick. Peter Claver cared for them. Many of those people became followers of Jesus.

? How did Saint Peter Claver follow Jesus?

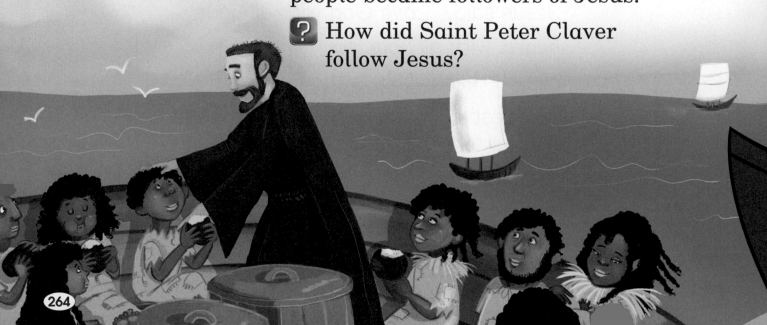

With Love and Fairness

Saint Peter Claver helped people in need. He treated them with fairness. He treated them with love.

 What are some ways you can act with fairness and love?

Activity On one ship, draw a picture of yourself acting fairly and with love. On the other ship, write two words that can be used to show love.

Faith Focus
What does it mean to live together in community?

Faith Words
community
A community is a group of people who respect and care for one another.

God's Family

A **community** is a group of people who respect and care for one another. People in a community help one another. In a community, everyone is needed. Everyone has something to give.

We all belong to the community of God's people. God makes each of us special. God blesses each of us with gifts and talents. We respect each other's gifts. God asks us to use our gifts to live as a community.

? How would you tell someone about a community?

Gifts and Talents

You are important to your family. You are important to your friends. You are important to the Church. You belong to the community of God's people.

❓ How are you important to your family, friends, and Church?

Activity

Gifts and Talents

Look at some of your gifts and talents. Tell how each one helps the people around you. In the space below draw or write what gifts you can share with others.

MAKING THINGS

TAKING CARE

CHEERFUL LAUGHTER

Catholics Believe

Religious Communities

Members of religious communities show us how to live the Great Commandment. These men and women make special promises or vows. Their vows help them to love God more than all else. Their promises help them to love other people and themselves.

Good Rules Help Us

Good rules help us to live together in a community. They help us to respect one another. The rules that a community makes are called laws.

Good laws help a community to live together in peace. Good laws help people to have the things that they need to live. Good laws help us to live God's Laws.

? What do we call the rules a community makes?

God's Laws Help Us

God's Laws help us to know right from wrong. They help us to make good choices. They help us to respect one another and to care for one another. They help us to treat people fairly and with respect. God's Laws help us to live as children of God.

? How do laws help us to live as children of God?

Faith-Filled People

Saint Louis

Louis was the ninth king of France. He wrote many good laws. These laws helped people to treat one another fairly.

Activity

Follow the road in the picture. Circle a favorite place. Write one way that you can live as a child of God there.

The Great Commandment

God wants all people to love him with their whole hearts. He wants all people to love and respect others as they love themselves. We call this the **Great Commandment.**

The Great Commandment helps us to live as the community of God's people. Jesus showed us how to live the Great Commandment.

Jesus gave us the gift of the Church. The Church helps us to live the Great Commandment.

? What is the Great Commandment?

Activity

Look at the pictures. Tell a classmate how the children are living the Great Commandment.

The Holy Spirit helps you to live the Great Commandment. He helps you to love God above all else. He helps you to treat others with justice and with respect.

I Follow Jesus

Activity

Living God's Laws

Finish each sentence. Write what you can do to live as a good member of your family, school, or parish.

_____

1. I can share my _____ .

_____

2. I can help by _____ .

_____

3. I can pray for _____ .

My Faith Choice

Look at what you wrote in the activity. Which one will you do this week? I will

_____

_____

Pray, "Thank you, Jesus, for teaching me the Great Commandment. Thank you, Holy Spirit, for helping me to live the Great Commandment. Amen."

1. The Great Commandment teaches us that we are to love God and to love other people as we love ourselves.

2. The Great Commandment helps us to follow Jesus.

3. The Great Commandment helps us to live as good members of our community.

Chapter Review

Recall

Find and circle the three words hidden in the puzzle. Share with a partner what each word tells about the Great Commandment.

GOD	LOVE	PEOPLE

L H L O V E T Y

Q L P G O D M U

P E O P L E B D

*Read each sentence. Circle **Yes** if the sentence is true. Circle **No** if it is not true.*

1. A community is a group of people who respect one another.

   Yes   **No**

2. Good rules help us to fight together in a community.

   Yes   **No**

3. All of God's Laws are good.

   Yes   **No**

Reflect

Why are communities important for us?

_____

- - - - - - - - - - - - - - - - - -

_____

Share Share with a classmate why he or she is needed in your school community.

Teach Me, Lord

The Bible has many prayers. This prayer is part of a psalm. Learn the words of this prayer by heart.

Leader   Lord God, help us to live the Great Commandment.

Reader   *Lord God, teach me your ways. You are my God and Savior.*

BASED ON PSALM 25:4–5

The word of the Lord.

All   **Thanks be to God.**

Leader   Keeping your Great Commandment means making a promise of love. Hear us, Lord, as we pray.
Wonderful! Wonderful for you!

All   **With all my soul, I will keep the promise of love.**

Leader   Wonderful! Wonderful for you!

All   **I will love my neighbor as myself.**

Leader   Wonderful! Wonderful for you!

(Share a sign of peace.)

With My Family

This Week . . .

In Chapter 20, "We Live as a Community," your child learned:

▶ Communities make laws to help people live together in peace. Good laws help us to live God's Laws. God gives us laws to help us show our love for God, for ourselves, and for other people.

▶ The Great Commandment is the summary of all God's Laws. The Church helps us to live God's Laws and the good laws that communities make.

▶ The virtue of justice helps us to treat everyone fairly. When we treat people fairly, we live the Great Commandment.

For more about related teachings of the Church, see the *Catechism of the Catholic Church*, 1877–1942, 1949–1974, and 2234–2246, and the *United States Catholic Catechism for Adults*, pages 307–309.

■ Sharing God's Word

Read together Matthew 22:34-40 about Jesus teaching the Great Commandment. Emphasize that the Great Commandment has two parts. We are to love God, and we are to love all people as we love ourselves.

■ We Live as Disciples

The Christian home and family is a school of discipleship. Choose one of the following activities to do as a family, or design a similar activity of your own.

▶ Good rules help us to live together. Talk about your family rules and how they help you to live together.

▶ Choose an activity to do this week to live the Great Commandment.

■ Our Spiritual Journey

The Ten Commandments are written on the heart of every person. They guide us toward living as God created us to live. They are the pulse of living the righteous life described in the Bible—that is, of our living in "right order" with God, with other people, and with all of creation. This week, pray as a family the psalm verse on page 273.

For more ideas on ways your family can live as disciples of Jesus, visit **BeMyDisciples.com**

Caring and Sharing

Our Lady of Mercy School has a "Caring and Sharing" group. The children and their families help sick and hungry people in the parish.

The Newman family has a new baby boy, Daniel. Daniel was born too early, before his body was ready. So he has to stay in the hospital until he is ready to come home.

Daniel's parents need to be at the hospital with him as much as possible. They won't have time to fix many meals. Daniel's parents will need help fixing meals for his older sisters.

WE REACH OUT

As Christians we reach out to people in need. We help one another. We care for people in our family and in our community.

Making Connections

Disciples of Jesus reach out to people in need. What can you do to help people in need?

with MATH AND SCIENCE

The families in your class are going to provide meals for Daniel's family on Tuesdays and Fridays. Daniel is going to be in the hospital for four weeks. One family from the class needs to volunteer for each meal. How many families need to volunteer to make a meal?

with LANGUAGE ARTS

Daniel is finally coming home from the hospital. You are going to make a banner to hang on his house to welcome him home. Write the words for your banner.

with CREATIVE ARTS

Play a game of charades. In pairs, role-play how you can help Daniel's family. Show what you can do to help Daniel's parents. Show how you can reach out in kindness to his sisters.

Faith Action

Write one way you can reach out to people in need. Tell your class.

_____

- -

_____.

Unit 5 Review

Name _____

A. Choose the Best Word

Complete the sentences. Color the circle next to the best choice.

1. The Great _____ is to love God with our whole heart and to love others as we love ourselves.

○ Commandment   ○ Prayer

2. We show people _____ when we treat them as children of God.

○ respect   ○ fear

3. The first _____ gathered together and showed how much they loved God and one another.

○ family   ○ Christians

4. The Great Commandment helps us to live as good members of our _____.

○ community   ○ team

5. The Ten Commandments teach us to _____ God.

○ respect   ○ disobey

B. Show What You Know

Match the two columns. Draw a line from the words in Column A to their meanings in Column B.

Column A

1. community
2. worship
3. honor

Column B

a. Give praise and honor to God
b. To treat people with great respect
c. People who care for one another

C. Connect with Scripture

What was your favorite story about Jesus in this unit? Draw something that happened in the story. Tell your class about it.

D. Be a Disciple

1. *What Saint or holy person did you enjoy hearing about in this unit? Write the name here. Tell your class what this person did to follow Jesus.*

_____

- -

_____

2. *What can you do to be a good disciple of Jesus?*

_____

- -

_____

- -

_____

The Good Shepherd

Shepherds take care of sheep. A good shepherd knows each sheep by name. The sheep come when they hear the shepherd's voice.

One day Jesus said to his friends, "I am the Good Shepherd. I know you all by name. I care for you. I love you so much I will give up my life for you. You are mine. You belong to me."

BASED ON JOHN 10:2–14

What I Know

What is something you already know about these faith words?

Heaven

_____

- -

_____

Parables

_____

- -

_____

Put an X next to the faith words you know.
Put a ? next to the faith words you need to learn more about.

____ Kingdom of God   ____ glory   ____ sin

____ Our Father   ____ charity   ____ joy

A Question I Have

What question would you like to ask about Saints?

_____

- -

_____

- -

_____

CHAPTER 21

Jesus and the Children

❓ How do people show that they are friends?

Jesus invites us to be his friend. Listen to what Jesus said,

"I have called you friends, because I have told you everything I have heard from my Father."

JOHN 15:15

❓ How do we know that Jesus wants us to be his friends?

Joy

We live with joy when we recognize that happiness does not come from money or possessions. True happiness comes from knowing and following Jesus.

The Church Follows **Jesus**

Read to Me

Children Helping Children

One cold day in France, a ten-year-old boy named Charles was out walking. He came upon another boy who was selling roasted chestnuts. Charles saw that the boy was not wearing shoes. Charles took off his own shoes and gave them to the boy.

Charles grew up and became a priest and then a bishop. In 1839, Bishop Charles traveled from France to the United States. He saw many poor children. Later, he asked children in France to help the poor children in the United States. This was the beginning of the Holy Childhood Association.

Today children all over the world pray and help children in need.

❓ **What are some ways that you can help other children?**

The Holy Childhood Association's Sister Merieti Riiki with children.

Activity

Helping Others

Look at each of the pictures. Write the ways the children in the pictures are being helped.

_____

- -

_____

_____

- -

_____

_____

- -

_____

_____

- -

_____

_____

- -

_____

_____

- -

_____

Share with a partner one way you or your family could help children in need.

Faith Focus
Why are all people so
special to Jesus?

Children of God

Jesus showed that every person is special. He showed that God loves everyone.

Jesus did amazing things. He made blind people see. He made people walk who could never walk before. He cured people who were sick. These were signs of God's love for people.

Jesus was kind and caring to people whom others did not like. He forgave people who sinned. He loved all people, even those who wanted to hurt him. Jesus treated everyone as a child of God.

? How did Jesus show that everyone is special to God?

"Love your enemies and do good to them."

Following Jesus

Everyone wanted to be with Jesus. People wanted to be near him. They followed him everywhere he went. Parents wanted their children to see Jesus and be near him too.

? Why do you think the people wanted to be with Jesus?

Catholics Believe

Children's Choir

Children help out in their schools and parishes. One way they help is by singing in the children's choir. This shows that children have a special work to do in the Church.

Activity

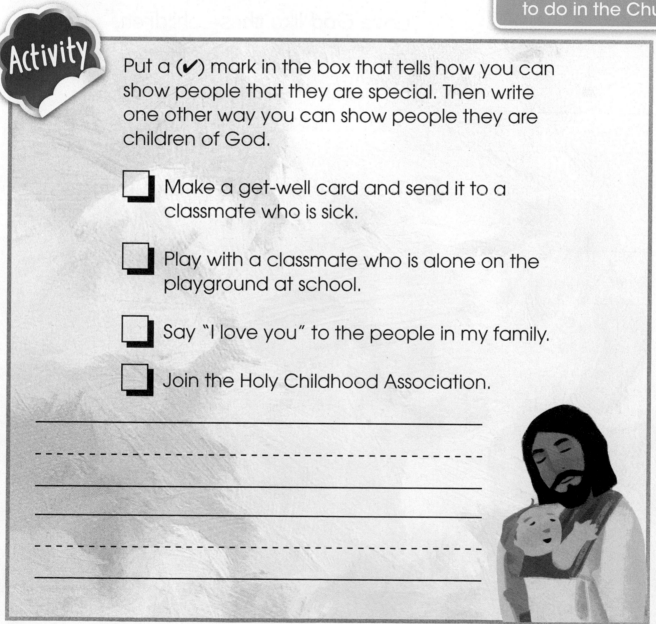

Put a (✔) mark in the box that tells how you can show people that they are special. Then write one other way you can show people they are children of God.

☐ Make a get-well card and send it to a classmate who is sick.

☐ Play with a classmate who is alone on the playground at school.

☐ Say "I love you" to the people in my family.

☐ Join the Holy Childhood Association.

_____

_____

_____

_____

Faith Focus
What did Jesus tell people about the Kingdom of God?

Faith Words
Kingdom of God
The Kingdom of God is Heaven. Heaven is happiness with God forever.

Jesus Welcomes Children

Here is a story from the Bible. It tells about Jesus inviting children to come to him.

People brought their children to Jesus. But the disciples told them to go away. Jesus said, "Let the children come to me." Then he blessed the children.

"Love God like these children," Jesus said. "Then you will be invited to live forever in the Kingdom of God."

BASED ON MARK 10:13–14,16

❓ What did Jesus do in the story?

Happiness with God

Jesus invites all people to come to him. All people are invited to live in the **Kingdom of God.** The Kingdom of God is happiness with God forever.

? What is the Kingdom of God?

Activity

Write a message telling a friend that he or she is special to God. Tell your friend why he or she is special to him.

_____

- -

_____

_____

- -

_____

_____

- -

_____

_____

- -

_____

You are special to God too. Draw yourself in the picture on page 286. Ask Jesus to bless you.

Faith-Filled People

Saint Nicholas

Nicholas tried to help children without being noticed. Many children around the world leave their shoes out on December 6, the day when we celebrate the feast of Saint Nicholas. They hope that Saint Nicholas will fill their shoes with treats.

We Are Children of God

In the Bible story, Jesus taught that all children are special to God. Some children have big, bright eyes. Others have happy smiles. Some are very quiet. Others talk all the time. All children are very different. Our differences show how special we are.

We treat all people as children of God. We do our best to live as children of God. We trust and love God with our whole hearts.

? Why are all the children in the pictures special to God? Tell a partner.

Jesus loves all children. Jesus loves you. The Holy Spirit helps you to share Jesus' love for others. True happiness comes from living as a child of God.

I Follow Jesus

Activity

Use words and pictures to make an "*I Care*" button.

I Care

My Faith Choice

Underline one way that you will treat others as children of God. This week, I will

1. invite a classmate to play with me.
2. tell my family I love them.
3. help out at home.

Pray, "Thank you, Jesus, for teaching me to treat others as children of God. Amen."

TO HELP YOU REMEMBER

1. God loves all people.

2. God wants all people to come to him.

3. God wants us to live in Heaven.

Recall

Use one of these words to fill in the missing word in each sentence.

Heaven	blessed	everyone	invites

_____

1. God loves _____.

2. The Kingdom of God is _____

3. Jesus _____ the children.

4. Jesus _____ everyone to follow him.

Reflect

How are you special to God?

_____

_____

Share	**Share with your teacher and family why you are so special.**

Let the Children Come

Our imagination can help us talk to Jesus and to listen to him.

1. Relax
Sit quietly in a comfortable position.
Ask God to fill your heart and mind.

2. Imagine
Imagine that you are going with your family to see Jesus.

3. Listen
Imagine that you are talking and listening to Jesus.

4. Think
Spend a minute quietly listening to what Jesus might be saying to you.

Thank Jesus for his love for you. Share this love with your friends and family.

With My Family

This Week . . .

In Chapter 21, "Jesus and the Children," your child learned:

▶ God loves all people and wants them to live with him forever in Heaven.

▶ Children of God share his love with one another.

▶ We live with joy when we recognize that happiness does not come from money or possessions. True happiness comes from knowing and following Jesus.

For more about related teachings of the Church, see the *Catechism of the Catholic Church*, 541–550 and 2816–2821, and the *United States Catholic Catechism for Adults* pages 67, 68, and 310.

◼ Sharing God's Word

Read together the Bible story in Mark 10:13–16 about Jesus blessing the children. Or you can read the adaptation of the story on page 286. Emphasize that Jesus invited the children to come to him and he blessed them.

◼ We Live as Disciples

The Christian home and family is a school of discipleship. Choose one of the following activities to do as a family, or design a similar activity of your own.

▶ Jesus welcomed everyone. He showed people that God loves them. As a family, do one thing that will show people that God loves them.

▶ Discuss the ways in which your parish welcomes children. Name activities, events, and opportunities that are available for children in your parish. Make an effort to participate in one of them.

◼ Our Spiritual Journey

In this chapter, your child prayed a prayer of meditation. This kind of prayer is also sometimes called guided imagery. Talk with your child about how our imagination can help us to pray and to be with Jesus. Prayer and imagination can help us talk and listen to Jesus. Provide a time and space for quiet prayer in your family. Visit a church together outside of Mass time and spend a few moments in quiet meditation.

For more ideas on ways your family can live as disciples of Jesus, visit **BeMyDisciples.com**

CHAPTER 22

We Are Children of God

? **What are some ways that people are different from one another?**

All people are unique. No two people are exactly alike. People have different personalities and talents. We have different skin, hair, and eye colors. We even speak different languages. The Bible, however, tells us that all people are the same in one important way.

God created man in his image . . .
male and female he created them.

GENESIS 1:27

? **How are all people the same?**

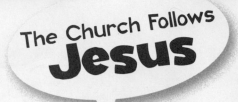

Disciple Power

Gentleness

Gentle people act calmly. They avoid actions that might lead others to anger or feeling hurt. They treat all people as children of God.

The Sisters of the Blessed Sacrament

Read to Me

Katharine Drexel cared for all people. She treated everyone as a child of God.

Saint Katharine began the Sisters of the Blessed Sacrament. The Sisters of the Blessed Sacrament work with African Americans and Native Americans. They work in schools and colleges. They work in cities and on the lands where Native Americans live. The Sisters of the Blessed Sacrament treat all people as children of God.

The Church honors Katherine Drexel as a Saint. We celebrate the Feast of Saint Katherine Drexel on March 3.

❓ What are some of the ways the Sisters of the Blessed Sacrament treat people as children of God?

Gentle People

The Sisters of the Blessed Sacrament continue the work of Saint Katherine Drexel. They teach others to treat all people with respect, fairness, and gentleness.

? What are some of the ways that you see people treating one another as children of God?

Activity

Work with a partner to show what the word *gentle* means. Act it out without any words.

Faith Focus
What does it mean to
be a child of God?

Faith Words
children of God
All people are
children of God. God
created all people in
his image.

Children of God

God created all people out of love. God created people in his image and likeness. God created all people to know, love, and serve him. God said that people should care for all creation.

All people are part of God's family. We are part of God's family. We are **children of God**. Children of God love God and love one another. Children of God are kind to others. Their kind words and actions show others that they love them and care about them.

? What do the pictures tell you about the children of God?

Care for Creation

Children of God care for everything God has made. The Bible says:

Great and loving God,
you make us to be like you.
You trust us to care for
everything you have created.
How wonderful you are!

BASED ON PSALM 8

Children of God take care of the water, air, trees, plants and animals. They take care of one another and all God's creation.

? How do you care for God's creation?

Catholics Believe

Blessed Sacrament

The Blessed Sacrament is another name for the Eucharist. We keep the Blessed Sacrament in the tabernacle. We bring the Blessed Sacrament to people who are sick so that they can receive Holy Communion.

Activity

Color the 😊 next to the actions that show that you care for God's people and all creation. Write one more way that shows you care.

😊 Recycle paper, plastic, and aluminum cans at home and in school.

😊 Turn off the lights when I leave a room.

😊 Talk to a friend while the teacher is talking to the class.

😊 Be a friend to someone who is lonely.

_____

😊 ------------------------------------

_____

God Gives Us the Gift of Life

God is our loving Father. God shares the gift of his life with us. The Bible says:

"Do you not know . . . that the Spirit of God dwells in you?"

1 CORINTHIANS 3:16

We are children of God. Children of God take very good care of the gift of life.

We can take care of the gift of our lives by taking good care of our bodies. We eat food that is good for us. We keep ourselves clean. We make choices that keep us safe. We get the rest we need. We get good exercise.

? What are some things children of God do to take care of the gift of life?

Care for Others

Children of God also respect and take care of the lives of other people. The Bible says:

> Care for one another. Always show respect for one another. BASED ON ROMANS 12:10

Children of God are kind to one another. We are gentle with others. We forgive others. We are fair. We are welcoming. We are peacemakers.

 **?** How can you help care for other people?

Caring for Self and Others

In one gift package draw or write how you can care for yourself. In the other gift package draw or write how you can care for someone else.

Faith-Filled People

Saint Josephine Bakhita

Josephine Bakhita was a young African girl. She was kidnapped and forced into the slave trade in Africa. When she was in her teens, she was left with the Canossian Sisters in Venice, Italy. There she came to know about God. Bakhita became a sister. She comforted the poor and encouraged others. Her feast day is February 8.

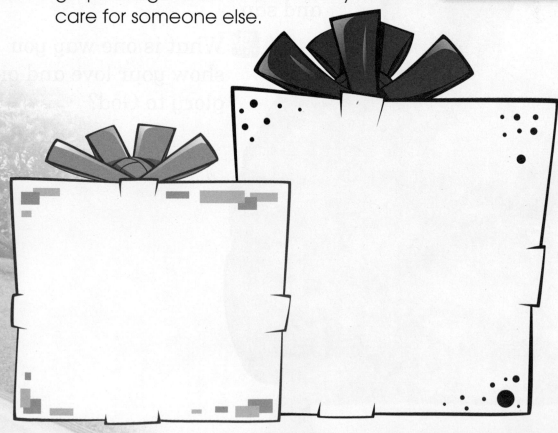

We Show Our Love for God

God created us to know and to love him. Jesus taught about God's love. He showed people God's love with his actions. He spoke to people about God's love. Jesus taught that God wants us to be happy with him now and forever in Heaven.

Jesus showed us how to love God. We show our love for God when we help other people. We show our love for God when we pray. When we take care of creation, we are showing our love for God.

We give **glory** to God when we do these things. Glory is another word for praise. Children of God give glory to God in all they do and say.

? What is one way you show your love and give glory to God?

God created you and all people to be children of God. The Holy Spirit helps you to treat all people as children of God.

I Follow Jesus

Activity

Being Gentle

Draw yourself acting in a gentle way. Share your work with a partner.

My Faith Choice

Check (✓) how you will live as a child of God. This week I will

- ☐ be kind.
- ☐ pray.
- ☐ help my family.
- ☐ care for God's creation.

Pray, "Thank you, Holy Spirit, for helping me to treat all people as children of God. Amen."

1. God created all people in his image.

2. God gives us the gift of life.

3. We are to take care of the gift of life.

Chapter Review

Recall

Use this number code. Find out the important message about yourself.

A	C	D	E	G	H	I	L	N	O	R	S	W
1	2	3	4	5	6	7	8	9	10	11	12	13

___ ___ ___ ___ ___
13   4   1   11   4

___ ___ ___   ___ ___ ___ ___
1   8   8   5   10   3   12

___ ___ ___ ___ ___ ___ ___ ___
2   6   7   8   3   11   4   9

Complete each sentence. Color the ○ next to the best word.

1. Children of God take care of the gift of ____ that God gives to everyone.

   ○ money   ○ life

2. We give ____ to God when we praise him because he is good.

   ○ glory   ○ blessings

Reflect

How can you care for the gift of life?

_____

- -

_____

Share   **Share with your class ways to help care for the gift of life.**

The Glory Be

All Christian prayer gives glory to God. Learn the Glory Be by heart. Pray it each day in English and Spanish. You can sing a joyful song of glory to God.

Glory be to the Father,
and to the Son
and to the Holy Spirit,
as it was in the beginning
is now, and ever shall be
world without end. Amen.

Here is the prayer in Spanish.

Gloria al Padre, y al Hijo y al Espíritu Santo.
Como era en el principio, ahora y siempre,
por los siglos de los siglos. Amén.

You can also sing God your glory.

Rise and shine
And give God the glory, glory,
Rise and shine
And give God the glory, glory,
Rise and shine
And give God the glory, glory,
Children of the Lord!

With My Family

This Week . . .

In Chapter 22, "We Are Children of God," your child learned:

▶ God created all people in the image and likeness of God. God created all people out of his infinite love.

▶ God calls all people to be responsible stewards of the gift of life. We are called to show our love for God, especially in the way that we treat other people.

▶ We are to care for and treat our own lives and the lives of all people with gentleness.

For more about related teachings of the Church, see the *Catechism of the Catholic Church*, 355–361 and 1699–1709, and the *United States Catholic Catechism for Adults*, pages 67–68.

■ Sharing God's Word

Read together 1 John 3:1. Emphasize that in Baptism, we are joined to Jesus and become adopted children of God. We are to live as Jesus taught.

■ We Live as Disciples

The Christian home and family is a school of discipleship. Choose one of the following activities to do as a family, or design a similar activity of your own.

▶ All people have the dignity of being children of God. Children of God love God and one another. Talk together about how your family can live as children of God. What kinds of words and actions show others that we love and care about them?

▶ Look through a children's magazine or picture book with your child. Point out all the pictures that show people living as children of God.

■ Our Spiritual Journey

Giving glory and praise to God is so important that we are reminded to glorify God as we are sent forth at the end of Mass. In the Concluding Rites, the priest blesses us in the name of the Father, and of the Son, and of the Holy Spirit. We are then sent forth to do good works, to praise and bless the Lord, with these words: "Go in peace, glorifying the Lord by your life." As a family, choose one thing you can do this week to glorify the Lord. Also, help your child to memorize the Glory Be on page 303 and pray it together daily.

For more ideas on ways your family can live as disciples of Jesus, visit **BeMyDisciples.com**

CHAPTER 23

Jesus Teaches about Love

? Which stories can you think of that help you to make good choices?

Jesus sometimes told stories to teach us ways to live as his disciples.

Jesus asked, "Who was the good neighbor in the story?" Someone replied, "The traveler who helped the man lying on the road." Jesus said, "You are right. Now, you treat other people the same way."

BASED ON LUKE 10:36–37

? What do these words from the Bible tell you about Jesus?

Disciple Power

Charity

Charity is loving others as God loves us. We practice charity when we love our neighbor as Jesus taught us.

Saint Frances Cabrini

Frances Cabrini always kept trying. People told her she could not be a nun, but she did. She asked other women to join her. Together, they helped people everywhere.

Frances was born in Italy. Frances sailed across the ocean and landed in New York City. She wanted to help the new people who had come to live in the United States.

Frances and the other women did good work. They built homes and schools for children. They built hospitals for sick people. They built convents where other women could learn how to serve God.

? How were Saint Frances and the other women good neighbors?

Living as Good Neighbors

Sometimes life was hard for Frances, but she prayed to God and worked harder. In 1917, Frances died in one of the hospitals that she had founded. All her life, Frances loved others as Jesus taught.

? How can we be good neighbors like Saint Frances and the other women?

A Good Neighbor

Look at the pictures. Who needs a good neighbor? Work with a partner to choose one of the pictures. Draw how you could be like Saint Frances Cabrini and be a good neighbor.

Jesus Teaches Love

Jesus' disciples called him "Teacher." In Jesus' time, this was a great honor and a sign of respect. As other teachers did, Jesus often used stories to teach.

One kind of story Jesus told is called a **parable**. A parable tells a story that can be used to help teach a lesson.

In a parable, the teacher compares two things. The teacher uses one thing that his listeners know well to help them understand the main point of the story.

❓ What is a parable?

Teaching through Stories

The parables that Jesus told helped his listeners to know and love God better. Jesus' parables also tell us how much God loves us. They show us how to live as good neighbors and as children of God.

? How does a parable help us learn?

Activity

Learning about Jesus

What words could you use to describe Jesus?

_____

_____

_____

_____

_____

_____

_____

Catholics Believe

Prayer of the Faithful

We are good neighbors when we pray for one another. Each Sunday at Mass we pray the Prayer of the Faithful. In this prayer, we pray for the Church, for the world, for people who are sick, and for people who have died.

Faith Focus
What does the
story of the Good
Samaritan teach us?

The Good Samaritan

The stories that Jesus told are in the Gospels. The Gospels are in the New Testament. Here is one story that Jesus told. He said,

One day a man was traveling down a road. Robbers hurt the man and took all his money. They left him lying on the road.

A religious leader came along. He saw the hurt man. He turned away and walked on by.

A little while later, a man who worked at the Temple came along. He saw the hurt man too. But he was in a hurry, so he walked on by.

? What do you think will happen next in this parable?

A traveler from Samaria saw the hurt man. The Samaritan stopped and put bandages on the man's wounds. Then he put the man on his own donkey and took him to an inn.

"Take care of this man," the Samaritan told the innkeeper. "I will pay you whatever it costs." BASED ON LUKE 10:29–35

? Why do you think Jesus told the story of the Good Samaritan?

Good Samaritans

Finish the picture story. Draw or write about how the children can act as Good Samaritans.

1.

2.

3.

Faith-Filled People

Saint Isidore the Farmer

Isidore spent much of his life working on a farm in Spain. He and his wife, also a Saint, showed their love for God by being kind to their neighbors. Although they were poor, Isidore and Maria shared their food with those poorer than they were. Isidore is the patron Saint of farmers and migrant workers. The Church celebrates his feast day on May 15.

A Good Neighbor

The Bible tells us:

Be kind and caring toward one another.

BASED ON EPHESIANS 4:32

The parable of the Good Samaritan helps us do what the Bible says. It helps us to live as followers of Jesus.

God wants us to love him and our neighbor as ourselves. God wants us to be kind and to care for people. God wants us to help people even when we do not feel like helping.

Jesus showed us how to care for one another. This story teaches us to be good neighbors to one an another.

? How can you be a good neighbor to someone?

You can be a good neighbor. You can show people how much God loves them and cares about them.

I Follow Jesus

Living as a Good Neighbor

Color a next to two ways that you can help someone this week as Jesus taught. Then write one other way that you can help.

☺ Say kind words to someone who is sad.

☺ Help to fold laundry at home.

☺ Give a get-well card to someone.

☺ _____

_____

My Faith Choice

I will do one of the things in the activity above. I will

_____

_____

_____.

Pray, "Thank you, Jesus, for teaching me to be a good neighbor. Amen."

1. Jesus told the parable of the Good Samaritan to help us to live as his followers.

2. God wants us to care for one another.

3. We show charity when we love our neighbors.

Chapter Review

Recall

*Read each sentence. Circle **Yes** if the sentence is true. Circle **No** if it is not true.*

1. Jesus told stories called parables.

   Yes   **No**

2. The Good Samaritan took care of the injured man.

   Yes   **No**

3. Jesus told stories to teach us to help others.

   Yes   **No**

4. The story of the Good Samaritan is called a fable.

   Yes   **No**

5. Neighbors are only the people who live next door to us.

   Yes   **No**

Reflect

What is a Good Samaritan?

_____

_____

_____

_____

Share Share with a partner ways your class can act as Good Samaritans at school.

We Pray for Others

We pray the Prayer of the Faithful at Mass.
We pray for other people.

Leader   Dear God, help us show love.

For the Pope and Church leaders, we pray to the Lord . . .

All   **Lord, hear our prayer.**

Leader   For our country's leaders, we pray to the Lord . . .

All   **Lord, hear our prayer.**

Leader   For people who are hungry, we pray to the Lord . . .

All   **Lord, hear our prayer.**

Leader   For people who are sick, we pray to the Lord . . .

All   **Lord, hear our prayer.**

Leader   Think of the people you wish to pray for. (Pause). We pray to the Lord . . .

All   **Lord, hear our prayer.**

With My Family

This Week . . .

In Chapter 23, "Jesus Teaches About Love," your child learned:

▶ Parables in the Bible help us come to know, love, and serve God.

▶ The parable of the Good Samaritan teaches us how we are to live as disciples of Jesus.

▶ We are to care about one another and to show our love by our actions as Jesus did.

▶ We practice charity when we love our neighbor as Jesus has taught us.

For more about related teachings of the Church, see the *Catechism of the Catholic Church*, 546, and the *United States Catholic Catechism for Adults*, pages 27–31, 79–80.

◼ Sharing God's Word

Read together the parable of the Good Samaritan in Luke 10:29–37. Or you can read the adaptation of the parable on pages 310–311. Emphasize that the Samaritan was a good neighbor because he stopped and took the time to help the injured man.

◼ We Live as Disciples

The Christian home and family is a school of discipleship. Choose one of the following activities to do as a family, or design a similar activity of your own.

▶ This week, when you take part in the celebration of Mass, help your child participate in the praying of the Prayer of the Faithful. After Mass, talk about the petitions that were used in the prayer.

▶ Talk about how your family can be good neighbors to one another this week. For example, help one another without having to be asked.

◼ Our Spiritual Journey

A Prayer of the Faithful is a prayer of intercession. Intercessory prayer is one of the Church's five main forms of prayer. In this chapter, your child prayed a Prayer of the Faithful. As the community of the faithful, we pray the Prayer of the Faithful at Mass or during the Liturgy of the Hours. Because these are the prayer intentions of the community and not of individual people, appropriate subjects for the prayer have a communal nature. Subjects may include the Church and her ministers, civil leaders, the world and its people, those who are sick or dying, those who have died, those who are grieving, and anyone celebrating a Sacrament. Read and pray together the prayer on page 315.

For more ideas on ways your family can live as disciples of Jesus, visit **BeMyDisciples.com**

CHAPTER 24

The Our Father

? Who has helped you to learn something new?

Many people help us to learn new things. Jesus taught his disciples how to pray.

> Jesus said, "Pray to God privately. God will see you and reward you. Speak from your heart and God will hear you. God knows what you need."

BASED ON MATTHEW 6:6–8

? What do these words from the Bible tell you about prayer?

Disciple Power

Humility

Humility helps us to know that all good things come from God.

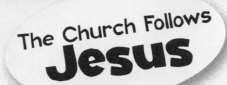

The Church Follows **Jesus**

Blessed Teresa of Calcutta

Read to Me

Mother Teresa of Calcutta showed us how important it is to pray. She once said, "Prayer brings our heart closer to God. If our heart is close to God, we can do very much."

Mother Teresa was very humble. She knew that praying often every day helped her to care for other people. Through a life of prayer and caring for others, she showed that God is everyone's Father.

Mother Teresa took care of people who had no one else. These people were very sick and very poor. They had no place to live. Mother Teresa fed them. She washed them.

The Church honors Mother Teresa as Blessed Teresa of Calcutta.

? What can you do to show that God is everyone's Father?

Activity

Pray Often

You can pray like Blessed Mother Teresa. You can pray often every day. Check your favorite time to pray.

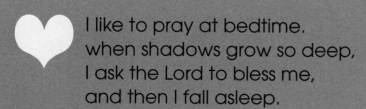

I like to pray at morning. God gives me the day to share with others in work and in play.

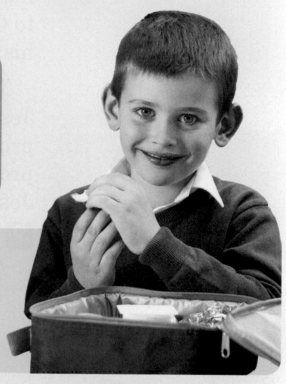

I like to pray at noon time when I eat my lunch. I like to say, "Thanks for the food. I love you, God, a bunch!"

I like to pray with family when we say our table prayer, and ask God for his blessing on the food that we will share.

I like to pray at bedtime. when shadows grow so deep, I ask the Lord to bless me, and then I fall asleep.

Jesus Prayed

Jesus prayed often. He talked to God his Father about everything. He listened to God the Father. He always did what his Father wanted him to do.

The followers of Jesus were with Jesus when he prayed. They saw him pray. They wanted to learn to pray as he prayed. They learned to pray from what Jesus did and said when he prayed.

? What did Jesus pray about?

The Church Prays

The Church learns to pray from Jesus too. We learn from reading and listening to stories about Jesus praying.

We also learn to pray from our family and the Church. We learn from listening to them and from watching them pray. We learn the words and actions of prayers.

 Which prayers have you learned to pray?

Faith-Filled People

Sister Thea Bowman

Sister Thea had the gift of singing. Singing was one way Sister Thea prayed. Everywhere she went Sister Thea sang about God's love for everyone. She praised God in everything she did. She lived the words of the Our Father every day.

Learning to Pray

In the picture frame, draw a picture of a person who has helped you to pray. Write the person's name under the picture.

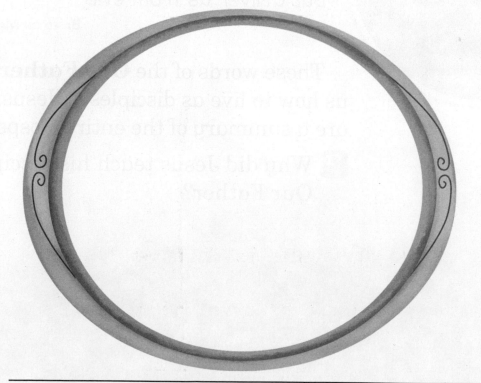

_____

- -

_____

Faith Focus
What prayer did Jesus teach us to pray?

Faith Words
Our Father
The Our Father is the prayer Jesus taught his disciples.

The Our Father

One day, one of the disciples asked Jesus to teach them to pray. Jesus said,

"This is how you are to pray.
Our Father in heaven,
hallowed be your name,
your kingdom come,
your will be done,
on earth as in heaven.
Give us today our daily bread;
and forgive us our debts, as we
forgive our debtors;
and lead us not into temptation,
but deliver us from evil."

BASED ON MATTHEW 6:9–13

These words of the **Our Father** teach us how to live as disciples of Jesus. They are a summary of the entire Gospel.

❓ Why did Jesus teach his disciples the Our Father?

Our Daily Bread

Think about the words "give us today our daily bread." These words ask God for what you need.

❓ What do you want to ask God for in your life?

Catholics Believe

The Lord's Prayer

The Lord's Prayer is another name for the Our Father. This is because Jesus our Lord gave us this prayer.

Activity

Asking God

In this space, draw one thing you need that you want to ask God to give you.

In this space, draw one thing you know that someone else needs that you want to ask God to give him or her.

Jesus Teaches Us to Pray

When we pray the Our Father, we tell God that we believe he is our Father. We honor the name of God. We trust him with all our hearts.

We ask God the Father to help us to live as his children. We ask for forgiveness.

We tell God that we forgive those who hurt us. We ask him to help us to do what is good. We pray that we will live with him forever in Heaven.

? What does praying the Our Father teach us?

Activity

The Lord's Prayer

The children in the picture are bringing the Lord's Prayer to life. In the space draw what you could do to live this prayer.

When you pray the Our Father, you show that you trust God. You show that everything good comes from God. You show that you believe that everyone is a child of God.

I Follow Jesus

Activity

Check where you can pray the Our Father.

- ☐ At Mass
- ☐ At Home
- ☐ On the school bus
- ☐ In the car
- ☐ In the park

My Faith Choice

This week, I will choose to live as a child of God. I will live the Lord's Prayer. I will

_____

_____

_____

Pray, "Thank you, Jesus, for teaching me to pray the Our Father. Amen."

1. Jesus taught us to pray the Our Father.

2. The Our Father is a prayer for all God's children.

3. The Our Father is also called the Lord's Prayer.

Chapter Review

Recall

Find and circle the words in the puzzle.
Use each word in a sentence. Tell a partner.

Jesus	Father	forgive	prayer

```
F O R G I V E T P
M C J E S U S W Z
O P R A Y E R K H
L P R F A T H E R
```

Color the hearts next to what we say to God when we pray the Our Father.

♡ *We tell God he is the Father of all people.*

♡ *We honor the name of God.*

♡ *We are afraid of him because he is God.*

♡ *We ask for forgiveness.*

♡ *We ask for help to live as his children.*

Reflect

How will you live the Our Father?

_____

- -

_____

Share **Tell a partner how you will live the Our Father in your life at home and school.**

The Our Father

Every day, Christians all around the world pray the Our Father. Pray the Our Father together.

All **Our Father, who art in heaven, hallowed be thy name;**

Leader Father, we call you by name and praise you.

All **thy kingdom come, thy will be done on earth as it is in heaven.**

Leader Father, we want to follow you and live as your children.

All **Give us this day our daily bread,**

Leader Father, we ask for your help

All **and forgive us our trespasses, as we forgive those who trespass against us;**

Leader Father, we ask for forgiveness, and we promise to forgive.

All **and lead us not into temptation but deliver us from evil.**

Leader Father, we pray that you will always keep us close to you. Amen.

With My Family

This Week . . .

In Chapter 24, "The Our Father," your child learned that:

▶ Jesus gave the Our Father to his first disciples.

▶ Jesus gave this wonderful prayer to all Christians of all times.

▶ Praying the Our Father teaches us to pray. It is a summary of the entire message of the Gospel.

▶ Humility is a virtue that reminds us of our right place before God. It helps us know that all we have is a gift from God.

For more about related teachings of the Church, see the *Catechism of the Catholic Church*, 2759–2856, and the *United States Catholic Catechism for Adults*, pages 483–492.

■ Sharing God's Word

Read together Matthew 6:9–13, the account of Jesus teaching the disciples to pray the Our Father. Or read the adaptation of the story on page 322. Emphasize that praying the Our Father honors God the Father and shows our trust in him.

■ We Live as Disciples

The Christian home and family is a school of discipleship. Choose one of the following activities to do as a family, or design a similar activity of your own.

▶ Practice saying the words of the Our Father with your child. When you take part in the celebration of Mass this week, help your child join in praying the Our Father.

▶ Use the Our Father as your mealtime prayer this week. Remember that the Our Father is the prayer of all God's children. Christians pray the Our Father every day all around the world.

■ Our Spiritual Journey

Saint Augustine called the Our Father the summary of the Gospel. Pray the Our Father as a prayer of meditation. Praying and living by the Our Father will create in you a pure and humble heart—a heart that keeps God and his love for you at the heart, or center, of your life. Make sure your children know this prayer by heart. As a family, go forth to live the Lord's Prayer!

For more ideas on ways your family can live as disciples of Jesus, visit **BeMyDisciples.com**

Children's Choir

The first graders at Our Lady of Guadalupe School are very excited. They have a special guest today, Mrs. Sanchez, the choir director.

Mrs. Sanchez has an important announcement for the first graders. She is going to start a children's choir. All children are invited to join.

The children will practice together. They will learn holy songs. Then they will sing at Sunday Mass. They will sing for others in the community too. When the children's choir sing, they will share God's love with others.

WE SHARE OUR GIFTS

We are all important members of the communities in which we live. Each of us has a responsibility to share our gifts with our families, school, parish, and communities.

Making Connections

Each of us is an important member of our school community. We are called to share our gifts with one another. The children's choir will share their gift of song to help the community praise God.

with LANGUAGE ARTS

Mrs. Sanchez has asked your class to make posters inviting all children to join the choir. What details or information will you need to include on the poster? Make the poster.

with CREATIVE ARTS

Learn the song, "We Sing Praise." Sing it to the tune of "London Bridge."

We sing praise to you, O Lord.
Wonderful are your works
We sing praise to you, O Lord.
And we love you.

with MATH AND SCIENCE

Sing the song above, "We Sing Praise." As you sing, clap and count how many syllables there are in each line. Then add the numbers together. How many syllables are in the song?

Faith Action

Write one way you can share your gifts with your school, and then do it.

_____

- -

_____.

Unit 6 Review

A. Choose the Best Word

Complete the sentences. Color the circle next to the best choice.

1. The Good Samaritan story teaches us that God wants us to _____ one another.

◯ respect   ◯ care for

2. God made all people _____.

◯ in his image   ◯ happy

3. God wants us to _____ Heaven.

◯ live in   ◯ remember

4. Mother Teresa was very _____.

◯ proud   ◯ humble

5. Jesus taught the disciples to pray the _____.

◯ Hail Mary   ◯ Our Father

B. Show What You Know

Circle the numbers next to the words that tell about the Bible story of the Good Neighbor.

1. parable   **4.** an innkeeper

2. a man from Samaria   **5.** care for one another

3. a camel

C. Connect with Scripture

What was your favorite story about Jesus in this unit? Draw something that happened in the story. Tell your class about it.

D. Be a Disciple

1. *What Saint or holy person did you enjoy hearing about in this unit? Write the name here. Tell your class what this person did to follow Jesus.*

_____

- -

_____

2. *What can you do to be a good disciple of Jesus?*

_____

- -

_____

- -

_____

The Year of Grace

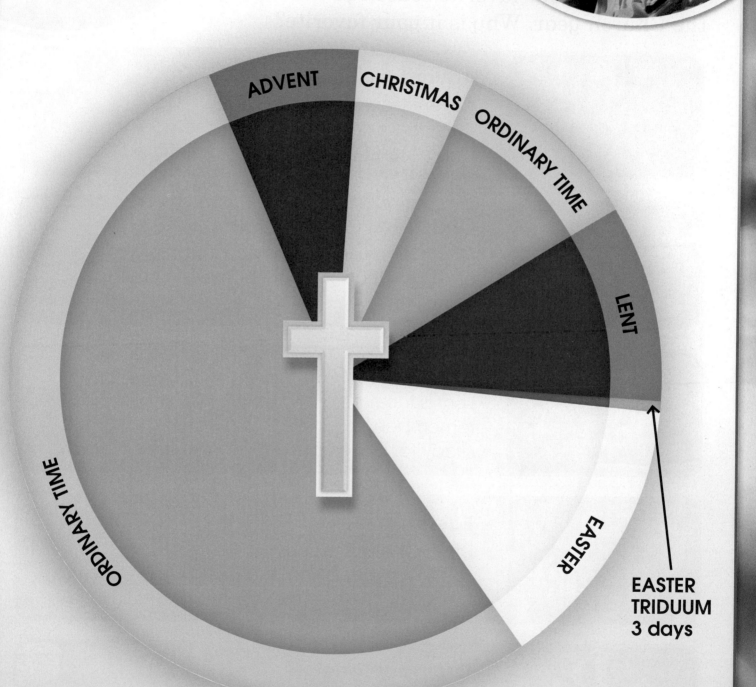

ADVENT

CHRISTMAS

ORDINARY TIME

LENT

EASTER

ORDINARY TIME

EASTER TRIDUUM
3 days

The Liturgical Year

The Church year of prayer and worship is called the liturgical year.

Check (✓) your favorite season or time of the Church year. Why is it your favorite?

Advent
Advent begins the Church year. We get our hearts ready to remember the birth of Jesus. The color for Advent is purple.

Christmas
At Christmas, the Church celebrates the birth of Jesus, God's Son. The color for Christmas is white.

Lent
Lent is the time of the Church year when we remember Jesus died for us. It is a time to get ready for Easter. The color for Lent is purple.

Easter
During the Easter season, we celebrate that Jesus was raised from the dead. Jesus gave us the gift of new life. The color for Easter is white.

Ordinary Time
Ordinary Time is the longest time of the Church's year. The color for Ordinary Time is green.

Exaltation of the Holy Cross

The Feast of the Exaltation of the Holy Cross celebrates the Cross of Jesus. The cross reminds us that Jesus loved us so much he gave his life for us.

Christians are people of the cross. We wear crosses. We have crosses in our churches and our homes.

Catholics begin and end almost every prayer with the Sign of the Cross. Our celebration of the Mass starts with the Sign of the Cross. Before we listen to the Gospel, we mark our head, mouth, and heart with the cross. We end Mass with a blessing and make the Sign of the Cross.

The cross shows that we belong to the Catholic Church. The cross shows that we belong to Jesus.

A Sign of Love

The cross is a sign of Jesus' love for us. Write Jesus' name and your name in the heart. On each of the other parts of the cross, write one way you can share Jesus' love with other people.

This week, I will show that I am a person of the cross. I will

_____

- -

_____.

Pray, "Jesus, help me to love you and your Cross. Amen."

Solemnity of All Saints

Saints are people who love God very much. They are holy people. They are members of our Church family who show us how to be good disciples of Jesus. Some Saints are adults. Other Saints are children. Saints come from all cultures and all nations. They live with Jesus in Heaven.

God wants each of us to become a Saint. We pray to the Saints to help us live as God's children. Mary, the mother of Jesus, is the greatest Saint. We pray to Mary too.

The Saints hear our prayers and want us to be happy with God. The Church honors all Saints on November 1 each year. This feast is the Solemnity of All Saints.

Mary, Saint Thérèse of the Child Jesus, Saint Andrew, and Saint Martin de Porres

The Greatest Saint

Draw a picture of Mary doing what God asks.
Also draw a picture of yourself helping Mary.

 This week, I will show my love for God by

_____

- -

_____

 Pray, "Mary, help me to love God and follow Jesus. Amen."

Advent

The Church season of Advent begins the Church's year. During Advent, we prepare for Christmas. We light candles to chase away the winter darkness. These candles remind us that Jesus is the Light of the world.

Jesus asks us to be lights for the world too. During Advent we let our light shine. We help people. We make gifts. We do secret good deeds for each other.

We gather in church and prepare our hearts to welcome Jesus. We sing and pray together. We remember that Jesus is with us every day.

My Light Shines

Decide what you can do to get ready for Christmas. Color in the flames to show what you can do.

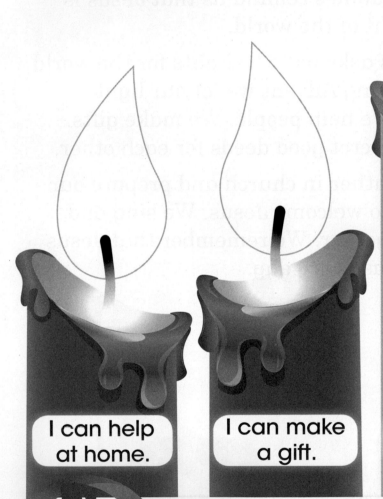

I can help at home.

I can make a gift.

I can help a neighbor.

I can pray.

During Advent, I will share the light of Jesus. I will

_____

- -

_____.

 Pray, "Jesus, you are the Light of the world! Amen."

Immaculate Conception

Mary is a very special mother. God the Father chose Mary to be the Mother of Jesus. Jesus is the son of Mary and the Son of God.

God blessed Mary more than any other person. The Bible tells us that God said to Mary,

"Most blessed are you among women . . ."

LUKE 1:42

God did this because he chose Mary to be Jesus' Mother.

God was with Mary in a special way all of her life. Mary was born without sin. Mary never sinned. This is what we mean when we pray, "Hail Mary, full of grace, the Lord is with thee."

We celebrate this special blessing God gave Mary each year. We celebrate the Immaculate Conception on December 8. We honor Mary and we honor God. We thank God for the special way that he blessed Mary.

Hail Mary

Tell Mary how special she is. Decorate the space around these words from the Hail Mary. Pray this first part of the prayer with your class.

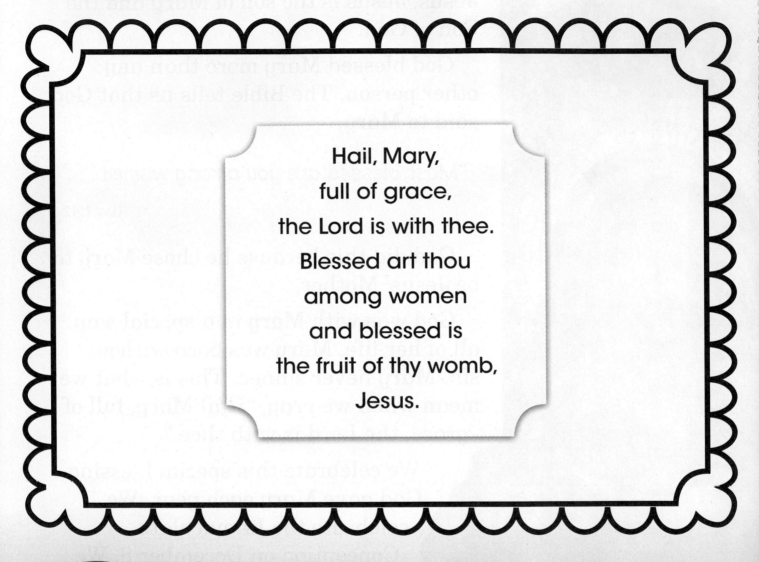

Hail, Mary,
full of grace,
the Lord is with thee.
Blessed art thou
among women
and blessed is
the fruit of thy womb,
Jesus.

This week, I will honor Mary. I will learn to pray the Hail Mary by heart.

Pray, "Mary, God loves you. I love you too. Blessed are you! Amen."

Faith Focus
Who does our
Blessed Mother
Mary want us
to love?

Our Lady of Guadalupe

Our Blessed Mother Mary loves all people. Mary told a man named Juan Diego how much she loves us.

Juan Diego lived in Mexico. One day as he was walking to Mass, Juan saw a lady. This lady was Mary.

Mary gave Juan a message to give his bishop. She wanted the bishop to build a church in her name. Mary gave Juan roses to show the bishop. Juan rolled the roses up in his cloak and took them to the bishop. When he opened his cloak, everyone was very surprised at what they saw. There was a beautiful image of Mary on the cloth.

The church that the bishop built is named Our Lady of Guadalupe. We celebrate the feast of Our Lady of Guadalupe on December 12.

Our Blessed Mother

Color the picture of Our Lady of Guadalupe. On the lines below the picture write, "I love you, Mary."

- -

This week, I will honor Mary. I will try my best to love others. Draw a ☺ next to the actions that you will do.

_____ Be kind to a friend.

_____ Help at home.

_____ Return crayons that I borrow.

 Pray, "Mary, Our Lady of Guadalupe. Help me to love God as you do. Amen."

Faith Focus
Why did the angels visit the shepherds?

Christmas

We like good news. It makes us happy. On the night of Jesus' birth, some shepherds heard good news. Angels said to them,

"Today in Bethlehem the savior God promised to send you has been born."   BASED ON LUKE 2:11

The shepherds hurried to Bethlehem. They found Jesus there lying in a manger, just as the angels said. The shepherds were Jesus' first visitors. They told others all that happened.

We want to welcome Jesus just as the shepherds did. We thank God for bringing joy that will never end. We share the Good News with others.

345

Las Posadas

People in Mexico celebrate the journey of Mary and Joseph to the inn in Bethlehem. The words *las posadas* mean "the inns." You can perform this skit with your class.

Mary and Joseph — In the name of God, can we stay here?

Innkeeper One — We have no room for you. We are too crowded!

Mary and Joseph — In the name of God, do you have room for us?

Innkeeper Two — We have no room here.

Mary and Joseph — In the name of God, do you have room for us?

Innkeeper Three — My inn is full. There is a stable in the hills. It is warm there.

Reader — *Read Luke 2:1–20.*

Leader — God our Father, we rejoice in the birth of your Son. May we always welcome him when he comes. Amen.

My Faith Choice

This week, I will treat others with love. I will

_____

- -

_____.

Pray, "May Jesus' birth bring joy, peace, and love to all people. Amen."

Mary, the Holy Mother of God

Gifts make us feel special. When someone gives us a gift, we know they care about us. God gave us the best gift. God the Father gave us Jesus, his Son. On Christmas we celebrate the birth of Jesus.

God the Father chose the Blessed Virgin Mary to be the mother of his Son, Jesus. Mary is the Mother of God. The Blessed Virgin Mary is our mother too. She loves and cares for all the children of the world.

We honor Mary, the holy Mother of God, in a special way on January 1. On this day, we go to Mass. We give thanks to God for the gift of our Blessed Mother. What a special way to start the New Year!

A Mother's Love

Our Blessed Mother did many things for her Son, Jesus. She does them for us too. Find the words in the border. Tell your class about times that mothers do these things. Then decorate the border.

Love

Teach

Holy Mary,
Mother of God,
Pray for us.

Pray

Protect

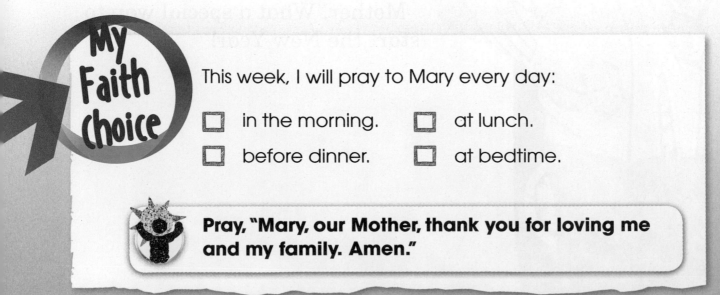

My Faith Choice

This week, I will pray to Mary every day:

☐ in the morning.   ☐ at lunch.

☐ before dinner.   ☐ at bedtime.

Pray, "Mary, our Mother, thank you for loving me and my family. Amen."

Epiphany of the Lord

During Advent, we waited and prepared for Christmas. We waited and prepared to welcome Jesus, the Son of God.

On Epiphany, we hear the story of the Magi. These wise men traveled a long distance to find Jesus. They went to Bethlehem and honored Jesus.

We want the whole world to celebrate the birth of the newborn Savior. We want Heaven and nature to sing and rejoice. Jesus is the Savior of the world.

We Announce the Birth of the Savior

Make the cover for a Christmas card. Draw a picture and use words. Tell everyone that Jesus is the Savior of the world.

The Magi honored Jesus. I will honor Jesus by

_____

- -

_____.

Pray, "Jesus, you are the Savior of the world! Amen."

Ash Wednesday

Prepare! That's what we do whenever something important is going to happen. Parents prepare for a new baby. They visit the doctor and get everything ready at home. Students prepare for tests so they can learn as much as possible.

The most important time of the year for the Church is Easter. Lent is the time when we prepare for Easter. Ash Wednesday is the first day of Lent. It is the first day of our preparation for Easter.

On Ash Wednesday, we go to church. The sign of the cross is made on our foreheads with ashes. We pray and ask God to help us to be more like Jesus. We ask God to help us celebrate Lent.

Being Like Jesus

Lent is a special time of prayer. In the spaces, put words or pictures to complete your prayer.

Dear God,

I praise and thank you for

I ask you to watch over

Keep them in your care.

Amen.

This week, I will remember to pray as Jesus did. I will

_____

- -

_____

 Pray, "Father in Heaven, thank you for helping me become more like your Son, Jesus. Amen."

Faith Focus
How does celebrating Lent help us to get ready for Easter?

Lent

Think about Spring. Remember how plants push their way up through the earth. Trees sprout leaves and buds. Birds sing their best songs.

During Spring, we plant new seeds. We cut away dead twigs and stems. We prepare for new life.

Jesus talked about death and new life. He held up a seed and said,

"Amen, amen, I say to you,
unless a grain of wheat
falls to the ground and dies,
it remains just a grain of wheat;
but if it dies, it produces much fruit.

JOHN 12:24

During Lent, we clear a place to plant seeds of faith and love. We work and pray. We grow in faith and love. We are getting ready for Easter.

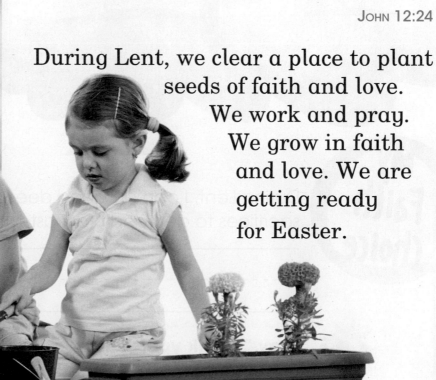

New Life

Put this picture story in order. Number the pictures from 1 to 6. Share the story with a friend. Tell how the story helps us to understand Lent.

My Faith Choice

During Lent, I can do good deeds and make sacrifices to get ready for Easter. I will

_____

- -

_____.

Pray, "Thank you, Jesus, for helping us to change and grow during Lent. Amen."

Palm Sunday of the Passion of the Lord

Sometimes important people come to our town or school. We go out and greet them. We cheer and rejoice!

Once Jesus came to the city of Jerusalem. He loved the people there. He wanted to gather them as a mother hen gathers her little chicks.

When Jesus came to the city, the people cheered. They waved branches from palm trees. They also spread their cloaks on the road to honor Jesus.

We remember this day at the beginning of Holy Week on Palm Sunday of the Passion of the Lord. On this day, we carry palm branches and honor Jesus too.

Honoring Jesus

These words are hidden in the puzzle.
Find and circle the words. Use the words
to tell a partner about Palm Sunday.

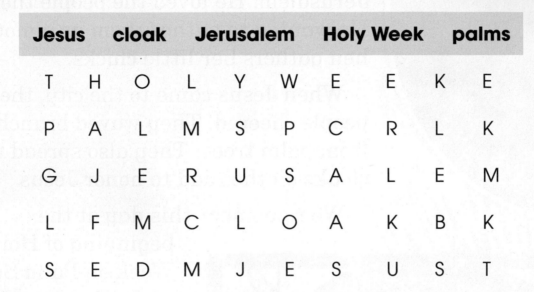

| Jesus | cloak | Jerusalem | Holy Week | palms |

```
T  H  O  L  Y  W  E  E  K  E
P  A  L  M  S  P  C  R  L  K
G  J  E  R  U  S  A  L  E  M
L  F  M  C  L  O  A  K  B  K
S  E  D  M  J  E  S  U  S  T
```

My Faith Choice

On Palm Sunday, the beginning of Holy Week, I can
honor Jesus. I will

_____

- -

_____

 Pray, "Hosanna in the highest! We rejoice and honor you, Jesus. Amen."

Holy Thursday

Holy Thursday is one of the most important days for our Church. On this day, we remember and celebrate the day on which Jesus gave us the Eucharist.

On the night before he died, Jesus celebrated a special meal with his disciples. We call this meal the Last Supper. At the Last Supper, Jesus took bread and said to the disciples, "This is my body." He also took a cup of wine and said, "This is the cup of my blood." Then Jesus said to them, "Do this in memory of me" (based on Luke 22:14–19).

We celebrate the Eucharist every time we celebrate Mass. When we do, we are doing what Jesus asked.

Thank You, Jesus!

Use the code to color the stained-glass window. Use the stained-glass window to tell what happened at the Last Supper.

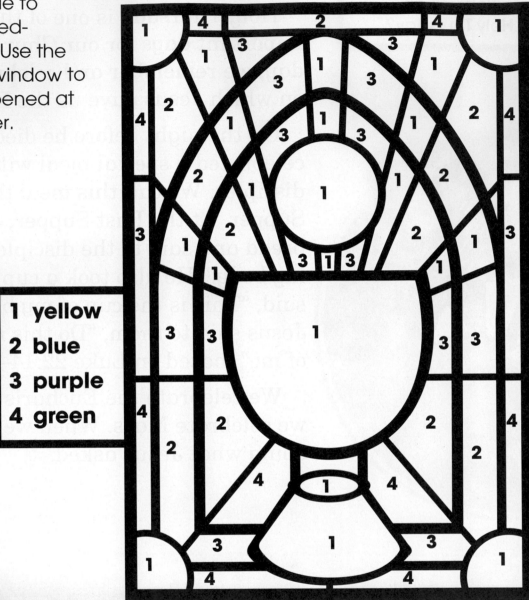

1 yellow
2 blue
3 purple
4 green

Jesus celebrated a special meal with his disciples and asked us to do the same. In Jesus' memory, I will

_____

- -

_____

 Pray, "Thank you, Jesus, for your gift of the Eucharist. Amen."

Good Friday

Sometimes we look at pictures or a gift that someone has given us. This helps us to remember and think about that person. What do you look at to help you remember someone?

The Friday of Holy Week is called Good Friday. It is a very special day for all Christians. It is the day we remember in a special way that Jesus suffered and died for us.

On Good Friday, the deacon or priest holds up a cross for us to look at. Looking at the cross, we think about and remember how much Jesus loves us. One way we show our love for Jesus is by loving one another.

Showing Our Love for Others

Draw a ✝ next to the ways you can show your love for others. Write one more thing you will do.

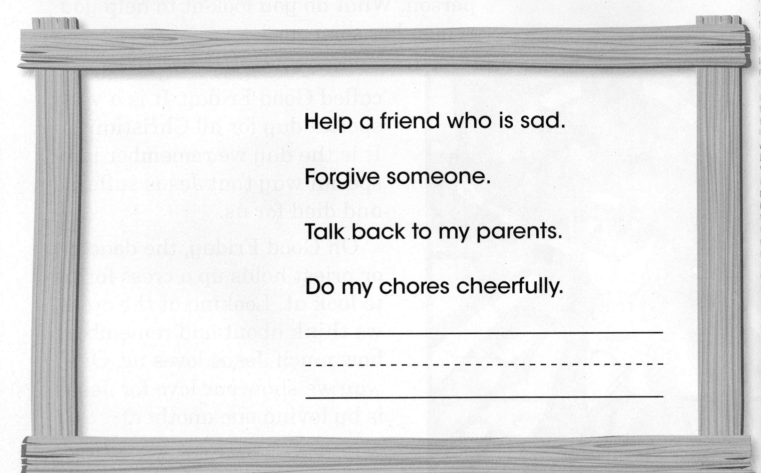

Help a friend who is sad.

Forgive someone.

Talk back to my parents.

Do my chores cheerfully.

_____

- -

_____

My Faith Choice

I will show that I am thankful that Jesus died out of love for us. I will

_____

- -

_____.

Pray, "We adore you and thank you, Jesus, for suffering and dying on the Cross for us. Amen."

Easter Sunday

At Easter, we see signs of new life all around us. These signs remind us that Jesus was raised from the dead to new life. We call this the Resurrection of Jesus. On Easter Sunday, Christians celebrate Jesus' Resurrection.

We are Easter people! Alleluia is our song! We sing Alleluia over and over during the fifty days of the Easter season. The word *Alleluia* means "Praise the Lord!" We praise God for raising Jesus from the dead to new life.

Every Sunday in the year is a little Easter. We sing. We rest. We enjoy one another. All year long we praise and thank God.

Praise the Lord

Decorate the Easter banner. Use colors and words about new life. Show your finished banner to your friends and your family. Tell them about the Resurrection of Jesus.

This week, I will give praise to the Lord. I will

_____

- -

_____

 Pray, "Jesus, you are risen. Alleluia!"

Ascension of the Lord

Forty days after Easter, Jesus led his disciples outside Jerusalem. He reminded them that he had suffered, died, and was raised to new life. Jesus said that we should share this Good News with everyone.

Then he blessed the disciples and returned to his Father in Heaven. The Church celebrates the day Jesus returned to his Father. We call this day the Solemnity of the Ascension of the Lord.

Sing to Heaven

Sing this song. Use the melody to "Frère Jacques." Teach the song to your family and sing it together.

He is risen. He is risen.
Yes, he is. Yes, he is.
He will come in glory.
He will come in glory.
Yes, he will. Yes, he will.

Sound the trumpet.
Sound the trumpet.
He ascends. He ascends.
We await the Spirit.
We await the Spirit.
Yes, we do. Yes, we do.

Holy Spirit, Holy Spirit.
Come to us. Come to us.
He will come and guide us.
He will come and guide us.
Yes, he will. Yes, he will.

Jesus asks us to share his Good News with others. I will

_____

_____

_____.

Pray, "Bless us always, Jesus, as we wait for you to come again in glory. Amen."

Pentecost Sunday

Sometimes we receive a gift that we use to help others. We have received that kind of gift from Jesus.

After Jesus returned to his Father, the disciples received the gift of the Holy Spirit. The Spirit helped them to share the Good News about Jesus with others. He helped them to do good work in Jesus' name.

On Pentecost Sunday, we remember that the Holy Spirit came to the disciples. We too have received the gift of the Holy Spirit. The Holy Spirit helps us to do good. When we do good things in Jesus' name, we lead others to Jesus.

The Gift of the Holy Spirit

Work with a partner and follow this maze. At each place, stop to share the Good News about Jesus with each other.

My Faith Choice

This week, I will honor the Holy Spirit. I will do good. I will

_____

- -

_____

 Pray, "Come, Holy Spirit, and fill my heart with your love. Amen."

Catholic Prayers and Practices

Sign of the Cross

In the name of the Father,
and of the Son,
and of the Holy Spirit. Amen.

Our Father

Our Father, who art in heaven,
hallowed be thy name;
thy kingdom come,
thy will be done
on earth as it is in heaven.
Give us this day our daily bread,
and forgive us our trespasses,
as we forgive those who trespass
   against us;
and lead us not into temptation,
   but deliver us from evil.
Amen.

Glory Be (Doxology)

Glory be to the Father
and to the Son
and to the Holy Spirit,
as it was in the beginning
is now, and ever shall be
world without end. Amen.

The Hail Mary

Hail, Mary, full of grace,
the Lord is with thee.
Blessed art thou among women
and blessed is the fruit
   of thy womb, Jesus.
Holy Mary, Mother of God,
pray for us sinners,
now and at the hour of our death.
Amen.

Signum Crucis

In nómine Patris,
et Fílii,
et Spíritus Sancti. Amen.

Pater Noster

Pater noster, qui es in cælis:
sanctificétur nomen tuum;
advéniat regnum tuum;
fiat volúntas tua,
   sicut in cælo, et in terra.
Panem nostrum cotidiánum
   da nobis hódie;
et dimítte nobis débita nostra,
sicut et nos dimíttimus debitóribus
   nostris;
et ne nos indúcas in tentatiónem;
sed líbera nos a malo. Amen.

Gloria Patri

Glória Patri
et Fílio
et Spirítui Sancto.
Sicut erat in princípio,
et nunc et semper
et in sæcula sæculórum. Amen.

Ave, Maria

Ave, María, grátia plena,
Dóminus tecum.
Benedícta tu in muliéribus,
et benedíctus fructus ventris tui,
   Iesus.
Sancta María, Mater Dei,
ora pro nobis peccatóribus,
nunc et in hora mortis nostræ.
Amen.

Apostles' Creed

(from the *Roman Missal*)

I believe in God,
the Father almighty,
Creator of heaven and earth,
and in Jesus Christ, his only Son,
  our Lord,

(*At the words that follow, up to and
including* the Virgin Mary, *all bow.*)

who was conceived by the Holy Spirit,
born of the Virgin Mary,
suffered under Pontius Pilate,
was crucified, died and was buried;
he descended into hell;
on the third day he rose again from
  the dead;
he ascended into heaven,
and is seated at the right hand of
  God the Father almighty;
from there he will come to judge the
  living and the dead.
I believe in the Holy Spirit,
the holy catholic Church,
the communion of saints,
the forgiveness of sins,
the resurrection of the body,
and life everlasting. Amen.

Nicene Creed

(from the *Roman Missal*)

I believe in one God,
the Father almighty,
maker of heaven and earth,
of all things visible and invisible.

I believe in one Lord Jesus Christ,
the Only Begotten Son of God,
born of the Father before all ages.

God from God, Light from Light,
true God from true God,
begotten, not made, consubstantial
  with the Father;
through him all things were made.
For us men and for our salvation
he came down from heaven,

(*At the words that follow, up to and
including* and became man, *all bow.*)

and by the Holy Spirit was incarnate
  of the Virgin Mary,
and became man.

For our sake he was crucified under
  Pontius Pilate,
he suffered death and was buried,
and rose again on the third day
in accordance with the Scriptures.
He ascended into heaven
and is seated at the right hand of
  the Father.
He will come again in glory
to judge the living and the dead
and his kingdom will have no end.

I believe in the Holy Spirit, the Lord,
  the giver of life,
who proceeds from the Father and
  the Son,
who with the Father and the Son is
  adored and glorified,
who has spoken through the prophets.

I believe in one, holy, catholic and
  apostolic Church.
I confess one Baptism for the
  forgiveness of sins
and I look forward to the resurrection
  of the dead
and the life of the world to come. Amen.

Morning Prayer

Dear God,
as I begin this day,
keep me in your love and care.
Help me to live as your child today.
Bless me, my family, and my friends
   in all we do.
Keep us all close to you. Amen.

Grace Before Meals

Bless us, O Lord,
   and these thy gifts,
which we are about to receive
   from thy bounty,
      through Christ our Lord.
Amen.

A Vocation Prayer

God, I know you will call me
for special work in my life.
Help me follow Jesus each day
and be ready to answer your call.
Amen.

Evening Prayer

Dear God,
I thank you for today.
Keep me safe throughout the night.
Thank you for all the good I did today.
I am sorry for what I have chosen
   to do wrong.
Bless my family and friends. Amen.

Grace After Meals

We give thee thanks,
   for all thy benefits, almighty God,
who lives and reigns forever. Amen.

Act of Contrition

My God,
I am sorry for my sins
   with all my heart.
In choosing to do wrong
and failing to do good,
I have sinned against you
whom I should love above all things.
I firmly intend, with your help,
to do penance,
to sin no more,
and to avoid whatever leads me
   to sin.
Our Savior Jesus Christ
suffered and died for us.
In his name, my God, have mercy.
Amen.

Rosary

Catholics pray the Rosary to honor Mary and remember the important events in the lives of Jesus and Mary. There are twenty mysteries of the Rosary. Follow the steps from 1 to 5.

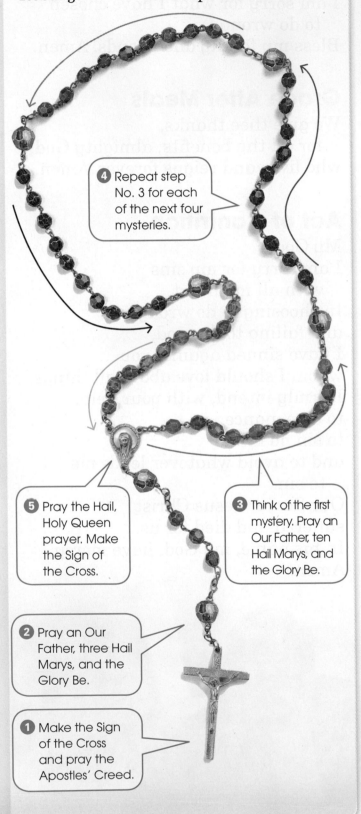

4 Repeat step No. 3 for each of the next four mysteries.

5 Pray the Hail, Holy Queen prayer. Make the Sign of the Cross.

3 Think of the first mystery. Pray an Our Father, ten Hail Marys, and the Glory Be.

2 Pray an Our Father, three Hail Marys, and the Glory Be.

1 Make the Sign of the Cross and pray the Apostles' Creed.

Joyful Mysteries

1. The Annunciation
2. The Visitation
3. The Nativity
4. The Presentation in the Temple
5. The Finding of the Child Jesus after Three Days in the Temple

Luminous Mysteries

1. The Baptism at the Jordan
2. The Miracle at Cana
3. The Proclamation of the Kingdom of God and the Call to Conversion
4. The Transfiguration
5. The Institution of the Eucharist

Sorrowful Mysteries

1. The Agony in the Garden
2. The Scourging at the Pillar
3. The Crowning with Thorns
4. The Carrying of the Cross
5. The Crucifixion and Death

Glorious Mysteries

1. The Resurrection
2. The Ascension
3. The Descent of the Holy Spirit at Pentecost
4. The Assumption of Mary
5. The Crowning of the Blessed Virgin as Queen of Heaven and Earth

Hail, Holy Queen

Hail, holy Queen, mother of mercy:
hail, our life, our sweetness,
    and our hope.
To you we cry, poor banished children
    of Eve.
To you we send up our sighs,
mourning and weeping
    in this valley of tears.
Turn then, most gracious advocate,
your eyes of mercy toward us;
and after this our exile
show unto us the blessed fruit
    of your womb, Jesus.
O clement, O loving, O sweet
    Virgin Mary.

The Ten Commandments

1. I am the LORD your God: you shall not have strange gods before me.
2. You shall not take the name of the LORD your God in vain.
3. Remember to keep holy the LORD's Day.
4. Honor your father and your mother.
5. You shall not kill.
6. You shall not commit adultery.
7. You shall not steal.
8. You shall not lie.
9. You shall not covet your neighbor's wife.
10. You shall not covet your neighbor's goods.

BASED ON EXODUS 20:2–3, 7–17

Precepts of the Church

1. Participate in Mass on Sundays and holy days of obligation, and rest from unnecessary work.
2. Confess sins at least once a year.
3. Receive Holy Communion at least during the Easter season.
4. Observe the prescribed days of fasting and abstinence.
5. Provide for the material needs of the Church, according to one's abilities.

The Great Commandment

"You shall love the Lord, your God, with all your heart, with all your soul, and with all your mind. . . . You shall love your neighbor as yourself." MATTHEW 22:37, 39

The Law of Love

"This is my commandment: love one another as I love you." JOHN 15:12

The Seven Sacraments

Jesus gave the Church the Seven Sacraments. The Seven Sacraments are signs of God's love for us. When we celebrate the Sacraments, Jesus is really present with us. We share in the life of the Holy Trinity.

Baptism

We are joined to Christ. We become members of the Body of Christ, the Church.

Confirmation

The Holy Spirit strengthens us to live as children of God.

Eucharist

We receive the Body and Blood of Jesus.

Penance and Reconciliation

We receive God's gift of forgiveness and peace.

Anointing of the Sick

We receive God's healing strength when we are sick or dying, or weak because of old age.

Holy Orders

A baptized man is ordained to serve the Church as a bishop, priest, or deacon.

Matrimony

A baptized man and a baptized woman make a lifelong promise to love and respect each other as husband and wife. They promise to accept the gift of children from God.

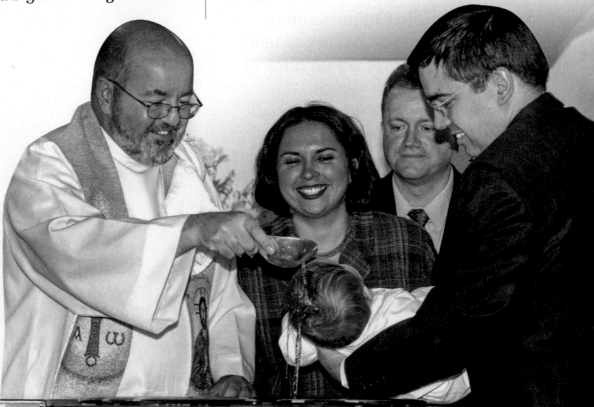

We Celebrate the Mass

The Introductory Rites

We remember that we are the community
of the Church. We prepare to listen to the Word of God
and to celebrate the Eucharist.

The Entrance

We stand as the priest, deacon, and other ministers enter the assembly. We sing a gathering song. The priest and deacon kiss the altar. The priest then goes to the chair, where he presides over the celebration.

Sign of the Cross and Greeting

The priest leads us in praying the Sign of the Cross. The priest greets us, and we say,

"And with your spirit."

The Penitential Act

We admit our wrongdoings.
We bless God for his mercy.

The Gloria

We praise God for all the good that he has done for us.

The Collect

The priest leads us in praying the Collect. We respond, "Amen."

The Liturgy of the Word

God speaks to us today.
We listen and respond to God's Word.

The First Reading from Scripture

We sit and listen as the reader reads from the Old Testament or from the Acts of the Apostles. The reader concludes, "The word of the Lord." We respond,

"Thanks be to God."

The Responsorial Psalm

The song leader leads us in singing a psalm.

The Second Reading from Scripture

The reader reads from the New Testament, but not from the four Gospels. The reader concludes, "The word of the Lord." We respond,

"Thanks be to God."

The Acclamation

We stand to honor Christ, present with us in the Gospel. The song leader leads us in singing **"Alleluia, Alleluia, Alleluia,"** or another chant during Lent.

The Gospel

The deacon or priest proclaims, "A reading from the holy Gospel according to (name of Gospel writer)." We respond,

"Glory to you, O Lord."

He proclaims the Gospel. At the end he says, "The Gospel of the Lord." We respond,

"Praise to you, Lord Jesus Christ."

The Homily

We sit. The priest or deacon preaches the Homily. He helps the people gathered to understand the Word of God spoken to us in the readings.

The Profession of Faith

We stand and profess our faith. We pray the Nicene Creed together.

The Prayer of the Faithful

The priest leads us in praying for our Church and her leaders, for our country and its leaders, for ourselves and others, for those who are sick and those who have died. We can respond to each prayer in several ways. One way that we respond is,

"Lord, hear our prayer."

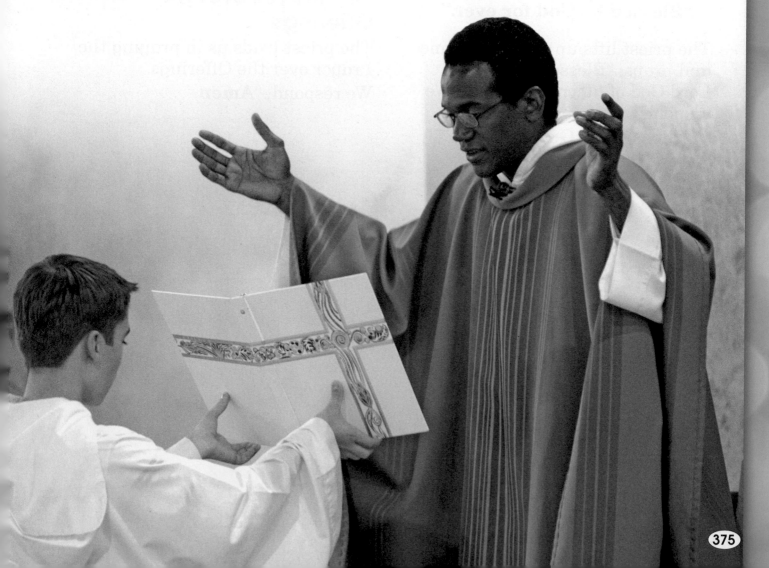

The Liturgy of the Eucharist

We join with Jesus and the Holy Spirit
to give thanks and praise to God the Father.

The Preparation of the Gifts

We sit as the altar is prepared and the collection is taken up. We share our blessings with the community of the Church and especially with those in need. The song leader may lead us in singing a song. The gifts of bread and wine are brought to the altar.

The priest lifts up the bread and blesses God for all our gifts. He prays, "Blessed are you, Lord God of all creation. . . ." We respond,

"Blessed be God for ever."

The priest lifts up the cup of wine and prays, "Blessed are you, Lord God of all creation. . . . " We respond,

"Blessed be God for ever."

The priest invites us,
"Pray, brothers and sisters,
that my sacrifice and yours
may be acceptable to God,
the almighty Father."

We stand and respond,

"May the Lord accept the sacrifice at your hands for the praise and glory of his name, for our good, and the good of all his holy Church."

The Prayer over the Offerings

The priest leads us in praying the Prayer over the Offerings.
We respond, "**Amen**."

Opening Dialogue

The priest invites us to join in praying the Church's great prayer of praise and thanksgiving to God the Father.

Priest: "The Lord be with you."
Assembly: "And with your spirit."
Priest: "Lift up your hearts."
Assembly: "We lift them up to the Lord."
Priest: "Let us give thanks to the Lord our God."
Assembly: "It is right and just."

After the priest sings or prays aloud the Preface, we join in acclaiming,

**"Holy, Holy, Holy Lord God of hosts.
Heaven and earth are full of your glory.
Hosanna in the highest.
Blessed is he who comes in the name of the Lord.
Hosanna in the highest."**

The Eucharistic Prayer

The priest leads the assembly in praying the Eucharistic Prayer.

We call on the Holy Spirit to make our gifts of bread and wine holy so that they become the Body and Blood of Jesus. We recall what happened at the Last Supper. The bread and wine become the Body and Blood of the Lord. Jesus is truly and really present under the appearances of bread and wine.

The priest sings or says aloud, "The mystery of faith." We respond using this or another acclamation used by the Church,

"We proclaim your Death, O Lord, and profess your Resurrection until you come again."

The priest then prays for the Church. He prays for the living and the dead.

Doxology

The priest concludes the praying of the Eucharistic Prayer. He sings or prays aloud,

**"Through him, and with him, and in him,
O God, almighty Father,
in the unity of the Holy Spirit, all glory and honor is yours,
for ever and ever."**

We respond by singing, **"Amen."**

The Communion Rite

The Lord's Prayer

We pray the Lord's Prayer together.

The Sign of Peace

The priest invites us to share a sign of peace, saying, "The peace of the Lord be with you always." We respond,

"And with your spirit."

We share a sign of peace.

The Breaking of the Bread

The priest breaks the host, the consecrated bread. We sing or pray aloud,

**"Lamb of God, you take away
the sins of the world,
   have mercy on us.
Lamb of God, you take away
the sins of the world,
   have mercy on us.
Lamb of God, you take away
the sins of the world,
   grant us peace."**

Communion

The priest raises the host and says aloud,

"Behold the Lamb of God,
behold him who takes away the
   sins of the world.
Blessed are those called to the
   supper of the Lamb."

We join with him and say,

**"Lord, I am not worthy that
you should enter under my
roof, but only say the word
and my soul shall be healed."**

The priest receives Communion. Next, the deacon and the extraordinary ministers of Holy Communion and the members of the assembly receive Communion.

The priest, deacon, or extraordinary minister of Holy Communion holds up the host. We bow, and the priest, deacon, or extraordinary minister of Holy Communion says, "The Body of Christ." We respond, **"Amen."** We then receive the consecrated host in our hands or on our tongues.

If we are to receive the Blood of Christ, the priest, deacon, or extraordinary minister of Holy Communion holds up the cup containing the consecrated wine. We bow, and the priest, deacon, or extraordinary minister of Holy Communion says, "The Blood of Christ." We respond, **"Amen."** We take the cup in our hands and drink from it.

The Prayer After Communion

We stand as the priest invites us to pray, saying, "Let us pray." He prays the Prayer After Communion. We respond,

"Amen."

The Concluding Rites
We are sent forth to do good works,
praising and blessing the Lord.

Greeting
We stand. The priest greets us as we prepare to leave. He says, "The Lord be with you." We respond, **"And with your spirit."**

Final Blessing
The priest or deacon may invite us,
"Bow your heads and pray for God's blessing."
The priest blesses us, saying,
"May almighty God bless you: the Father, and the Son, and the Holy Spirit."
We respond, **"Amen."**

Dismissal of the People
The priest or deacon sends us forth, using these or similar words,
"Go in peace, glorifying the Lord by your life."
We respond,
"Thanks be to God."
We sing a hymn. The priest and the deacon kiss the altar. The priest, deacon, and other ministers bow to the altar and leave in procession.

The Sacrament of Penance and Reconciliation

Individual Rite
Greeting
Scripture Reading
Confession of Sins
    and Acceptance of Penance
Act of Contrition
Absolution
Closing Prayer

Communal Rite
Greeting
Scripture Reading
Homily
Examination of Conscience, a
    Litany of Contrition, and the
    Lord's Prayer
Individual Confession and Absolution
Closing Prayer

A Visit to Church

Catholic churches are built in many styles and sizes. Some Catholic churches are older and some are newer. Some are big and some are small. But, all churches are places where people worship God.

Baptismal Font

As you enter a Catholic church, you may see a baptismal font. The baptismal font is the pool of water used for the Sacrament of Baptism. Water is used to remind us of new life.

Ambo

The ambo is the special place from where the Word of God, the Scriptures, is read. The lector is the person who reads the first and second readings during Mass. The deacon or priest reads the Gospel.

Paschal Candle

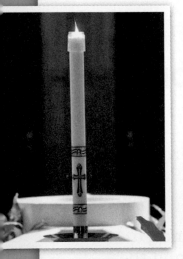

During the Easter Season, the Paschal candle, also called the Easter candle, is placed near the baptismal font. It reminds us of Jesus, the Light of the world.

Assembly

The assembly is the people gathered for Mass. The pews are the seats where the people sit.

The Book of the Gospels Lectionary

The Book of the Gospels contains the Gospel readings we listen to at Mass. The first two readings are read from the Lectionary.

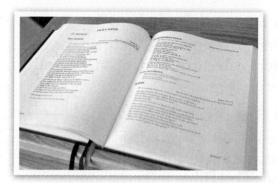

Crucifix

You will see a crucifix or cross that might be carried in procession by one of the servers. Or, it might be a crucifix or cross hanging from the ceiling or hung on the wall.

Tabernacle

The tabernacle is the place in the church where the Eucharist or Blessed Sacrament is kept. Some churches have a chapel where people can pray. When the candle next to the tabernacle is lit, it means that the Blessed Sacrament is in the tabernacle.

Altar

The altar is where the Liturgy of the Eucharist is celebrated at Mass. It reminds us of the Last Supper and that Jesus died for us. It is the table from which Jesus shares his Body and Blood with us.

It is very important to remember that through the Church, Christ continues to be with us in the world. The Church is every one of us, the People of God.

Key Teachings of the Catholic Church

The Mystery of God

Divine Revelation

Who am I?

You are a person created by God. God wants you to live in friendship with him on Earth and forever in Heaven.

How do we know this about ourselves?

God knows and loves all people. God wants us to know and love him too. God tells us about ourselves. God also tells us about himself.

How did God tell us?

God tells us in many ways. First, all the things God has created tell us about him. We see God's goodness and beauty in creation. Second, God came to us and he told us about himself. He told us the most when he sent his Son, Jesus Christ. God's Son became one of us and lived among us. He showed us who God is.

What is faith?

Faith is a gift from God. It helps us to know and to believe in God.

What is a mystery of faith?

A mystery of faith can never be known completely. We cannot know everything about God. We only know who God is because he told us about himself.

What is Divine Revelation?

God wants us to know about him. Divine Revelation is how he freely makes himself known to us. God has told us about himself and his plan for us. He has done this so that we can live in friendship with him and with one another forever.

What is Sacred Tradition?

The word *tradition* means "to pass on." The Church's Sacred Tradition passes on what God has told us. The Holy Spirit guides the Church to tell us about God.

Sacred Scripture

What is Sacred Scripture?

Sacred Scripture means "holy writings." Sacred Scripture are writings that tell God's story.

What is the Bible?

The Bible is God's Word. It is a holy book. The stories in the Bible teach about God. The Bible tells the stories about Jesus. When you listen to the Bible, you are listening to God.

What does it mean to say that the Bible is inspired?

This means that the Holy Spirit helped people write about God. The Holy Spirit helped the writers tell what God wants us to know about him.

What is the Old Testament?

The Old Testament is the first part of the Bible. It has forty-six books. They were written before the birth of Jesus. The Old Testament tells the story of creation. It tells about Adam and Eve. It tells about the promise, or Covenant, between God and his people.

What is the Covenant?

The Covenant is the promise that God and his people freely made. It is God's promise always to love and be kind to his people.

What are the writings of the prophets?

God chose people to speak in his name. These people are called the prophets. We read the message of the prophets in the Bible. The prophets remind God's people that God is faithful. They remind God's people to be faithful to the Covenant.

What is the New Testament?

The New Testament is the second part of the Bible. It has twenty-seven books. These books were inspired by the Holy Spirit. They were written during the time of the Apostles. They are about Jesus Christ. They tell about his saving work.

What are the Gospels?

The Gospels are the four books at the beginning of the New Testament. They tell the story of Jesus and his teachings. The four Gospels are Matthew, Mark, Luke, and John.

What are the letters of Saint Paul?

The letters of Saint Paul are in the New Testament. The letters teach about the Church. They tell how to follow Jesus. Some of these letters were written before the Gospels.

The Holy Trinity

Who is the Mystery of the Holy Trinity?

The Holy Trinity is the mystery of One God in Three Persons—God the Father, God the Son, and God the Holy Spirit.

Who is God the Father?

God the Father is the First Person of the Holy Trinity.

Who is God the Son?

God the Son is Jesus Christ. He is the Second Person of the Holy Trinity. God the Father sent his Son to be one of us and live with us.

Who is God the Holy Spirit?

The Holy Spirit is the Third Person of the Holy Trinity. God sends us the Holy Spirit to help us to know and love God better. The Holy Spirit helps us live as children of God.

Divine Work of Creation

What does it mean to call God the Creator?

God is the Creator. He has made everyone and everything out of love. He has created everyone and everything without any help.

Who are angels?

Angels are spiritual beings. They do not have bodies like we do. Angels give glory to God at all times. They sometimes serve God by bringing his message to people.

Why are human beings special?

God creates every human being in his image and likeness. God shares his life with us. God wants us to be happy with him forever.

What is the soul?

The soul is the spiritual part of a person. The soul will never die. It is the part of us that lives forever. It bears the image of God.

What is free will?

Free will is the power God gives us to choose between good and evil. Free will gives us the power to turn toward God.

What is Original Sin?

Original Sin is the sin of Adam and Eve. They chose to disobey God. As a result of Original Sin, death, sin, and suffering came into the world.

Jesus Christ, Son of God, Son of Mary

What is the Annunciation?

At the Annunciation, the angel Gabriel came to Mary. The angel had a message for her. God had chosen her to be the Mother of his Son, Jesus.

What is the Incarnation?

The Incarnation is the Son of God becoming a man and still being God. Jesus Christ is true God and true man.

What does it mean that Jesus is Lord?

The word *lord* means "master or ruler." When we call Jesus "Lord," we mean that he is truly God.

What is the Paschal Mystery?

The Paschal Mystery is the Passion, Death, Resurrection, and Ascension of Jesus Christ. Jesus passed over from death into new and glorious life.

What is Salvation?

The word *salvation* means "to save." It is the saving of all people from sin and death through Jesus Christ.

What is the Resurrection?

The Resurrection is God's raising Jesus from the dead to new life.

What is the Ascension?

The Ascension is the return of the Risen Jesus to his Father in Heaven.

What is the Second Coming of Christ?

Christ will come again in glory at the end of time. This is the Second Coming of Christ. He will judge the living and the dead. This is the fulfillment of God's plan.

What does it mean that Jesus is the Messiah?

The word *messiah* means "anointed one." He is the Messiah. God promised to send the Messiah to save all people. Jesus is the Savior of the world.

The Mystery of the Church

What is the Church?

The word *church* means "those who are called together." The Church is the Body of Christ. It is the new People of God.

What does the Church do?

The Church tells all people the Good News of Jesus Christ. The Church invites all people to know, love, and serve Jesus.

What is the Body of Christ?

The Church is the Body of Christ on Earth. Jesus Christ is the Head of the Church and all baptized people are its members.

Who are the People of God?

The Church is the People of God. God invites all people to belong to the People of God. The People of God live as one family in God.

What is the Communion of Saints?

The Communion of Saints is all of the holy people that make up the Church. It is the faithful followers of Jesus on Earth. It is those who have died who are still becoming holier. It is also those who have died and are happy forever with God in Heaven.

What are the Marks of the Church?

There are four main ways to describe the Church. We call these the four Marks of the Church. The Church is one, holy, catholic, and apostolic.

Who are the Apostles?

The Apostles were the disciples whom Jesus chose. He sent them to preach the Gospel to the whole world in his name. Some of their names are Peter, Andrew, James, and John.

What is Pentecost?

Pentecost is the day the Holy Spirit came to the disciples of Jesus. This happened fifty days after the Resurrection. The work of the Church began on this day.

Who are the clergy?

The clergy are bishops, priests, and deacons. They have received the Sacrament of Holy Orders. They serve the whole Church.

What is the work of the Pope?

Jesus Christ is the true Head of the Church. The Pope and the bishops lead the Church in his name. The Pope is the bishop of Rome. He is the successor to Saint Peter the Apostle, the first Pope. The pope brings the Church together. The Holy Spirit guides the Pope when he speaks about faith and about what Catholics believe.

What is the work of the bishops?

The other bishops are the successors of the other Apostles. They teach and lead the Church in their dioceses. The Holy Spirit always guides the Pope and all of the bishops. He guides them when they make important decisions.

What is religious life?

Some men and women want to follow Jesus in a special way. They choose the religious life. They promise not to marry. They dedicate their whole lives to doing Jesus' work. They promise to live holy lives. They promise to live simply. They share what they have with others. They live together in groups and they promise to obey the rules of their community. They may lead quiet lives of prayer, or teach, or take care of people who are sick or poor.

Who are laypeople?

Many people do not receive the Sacrament of Holy Orders. Many are not members of a religious community. These are laypeople. Laypeople follow Christ every day by what they do and say.

The Blessed Virgin Mary

Who is Mary?

God chose Mary to be the mother of his only Son, Jesus. Mary is the Mother of God. She is the Mother of Jesus. She is the Mother of the Church. Mary is the greatest Saint.

What is the Immaculate Conception?

From the first moment of her being, Mary was preserved from sin. This special grace from God continued throughout her whole life. We call this the Immaculate Conception.

What is the Assumption of Mary?

At the end of her life on Earth, the Blessed Virgin Mary was taken body and soul into Heaven. Mary hears our prayers. She tells her Son what we need. She reminds us of the life that we all hope to share when Christ, her Son, comes again in glory.

Life Everlasting

What is eternal life?

Eternal life is life after death. At death the soul leaves the body. It passes into eternal life.

What is Heaven?

Heaven is living with God and with Mary and all the Saints in happiness forever after we die.

What is the Kingdom of God?

The Kingdom of God is also called the Kingdom of Heaven. It is all people and creation living in friendship with God.

What is Purgatory?

Purgatory is the chance to grow in love for God after we die so we can live forever in heaven.

What is hell?

Hell is life away from God and the Saints forever after death.

Celebration of the Christian Life and Mystery

Liturgy and Worship

What is worship?

Worship is the praise we give God. The Church worships God in the liturgy.

What is liturgy?

The liturgy is the Church's worship of God. It is the work of the Body of Christ. Christ is present by the power of the Holy Spirit.

What is the liturgical year?

The liturgical year is the name of the seasons and feasts that make up the Church year of worship. The main seasons of the Church year are Advent, Christmas, Lent, and Easter. The Triduum is the three holy days just before Easter. The rest of the liturgical year is called Ordinary Time.

The Sacraments

What are the Sacraments?

The Sacraments are the seven signs of God's love for us that Jesus gave the Church. We share in God's love when we celebrate the sacraments.

What are the Sacraments of Christian Initiation?

The Sacraments of Christian Initiation are Baptism, Confirmation, and Eucharist.

What is the Sacrament of Baptism?

Baptism joins us to Christ. It makes us members of the Church. We receive the gift of the Holy Spirit. Original Sin and our personal sins are forgiven. Through Baptism, we belong to Christ.

What is the Sacrament of Confirmation?

At Confirmation we receive the gift of the Holy Spirit. The Holy Spirit strengthens us to live our Baptism.

What is the Sacrament of Eucharist?

In the Eucharist, we join with Christ. We give thanksgiving, honor, and glory to God the Father. Through the power of the Holy Spirit, the bread and wine become the Body and Blood of Jesus Christ.

Why do we have to participate at Sunday Mass?

Catholics participate in the Eucharist on Sundays and holy days of obligation. Sunday is the Lord's Day. Participating at the Mass and receiving Holy Communion, the Body and Blood of Christ, when we are old enough, are necessary for Catholics.

What is the Mass?

The Mass is the main celebration of the Church. At Mass we worship God. We listen to God's Word. We celebrate and share in the Eucharist.

What are the Sacraments of Healing?

The two Sacraments of Healing are the Sacrament of Penance and Reconciliation and the Sacrament of the Anointing of the Sick.

What is confession?

Confession is telling our sins to a priest in the Sacrament of Penance and Reconciliation. Confession is another name for the Sacrament.

What is contrition?

Contrition is being truly sorry for our sins. We want to make up for the hurt our sins have caused. We do not want to sin again.

What is penance?

A penance is a prayer or act of kindness. The penance we do shows that we are truly sorry for our sins. The priest gives us a penance to help repair the hurt caused by our sin.

What is absolution?

Absolution is the forgiveness of sins by God through the words and actions of the priest.

What is the Sacrament of the Anointing of the Sick?

The Sacrament of the Anointing of the Sick is one of the two Sacraments of Healing. We receive this Sacrament when we are very sick, old, or dying. This Sacrament helps make our faith and trust in God strong.

What are the Sacraments at the Service of Communion?

Holy Orders and Matrimony, or Marriage, are the two Sacraments at the Service of Communion. People who receive these Sacraments serve God.

What is the Sacrament of Holy Orders?

In this Sacrament, baptized men are consecrated as bishops, priests, or deacons. They serve the whole Church. They serve in the name and person of Christ.

Who is a bishop?

A bishop is a priest. He receives the fullness of the Sacrament of Holy Orders. He is a successor to the Apostles. He leads and serves in a diocese. He teaches and leads worship in the name of Jesus.

Who is a priest?

A priest is a baptized man who receives the Sacrament of Holy Orders. Priests work with their bishops. The priest teaches about the Catholic faith. He celebrates Mass. Priests help to guide the Church.

Who is a deacon?

A deacon is ordained to help bishops and priests. He is not a priest. He is ordained to serve the Church.

What is the Sacrament of Matrimony?

In the Sacrament of Matrimony, or Marriage, a baptized man and a baptized woman make a lifelong promise. They promise to serve the Church as a married couple. They promise to love each other. They show Christ's love to others.

What are the sacramentals of the Church?

Sacramentals are objects and blessings the Church uses. They help us worship God.

Life in the Spirit

The Moral Life

Why did God create us?

God created us to give honor and glory to him. God created us to live a life of blessing with him here on Earth and forever in Heaven.

What does it mean to live a moral life?

God wants us to be happy. He gives us the gift of his grace. When we accept God's gift by living the way Jesus taught us, we are being moral.

What is the Great Commandment?

Jesus taught us to love God above all else. He taught us to love our neighbors as ourselves. This is the path to happiness.

What are the Ten Commandments?

The Ten Commandments are the laws that God gave Moses. They teach us to live as God's people. They teach us to love God, others, and ourselves.

The Commandments are written on the hearts of all people.

What are the Beatitudes?

The Beatitudes are teachings of Jesus. They tell us what real happiness is. The Beatitudes tell us about the Kingdom of God. They help us live as followers of Jesus. They help us keep God at the center of our lives.

What are the Works of Mercy?

God's love and kindness is at work in the world. This is what mercy is. Human works of mercy are acts of loving kindness. We reach out to people. We help them with what they need for their bodies and their spirits.

What are the Precepts of the Church?

The Precepts of the Church are five rules. These rules help us worship God and grow in love of God and our neighbors.

Holiness of Life and Grace

What is holiness?

Holiness is life with God. Holy people are in the right relationship with God, with people, and with all of creation.

What is grace?

Grace is the gift of God sharing his life and love with us.

What is sanctifying grace?

Sanctifying grace is the grace we receive at Baptism. It is a free gift of God, given by the Holy Spirit.

What are the Gifts of the Holy Spirit?

The seven Gifts of the Holy Spirit help us to live our Baptism. They are wisdom, understanding, right judgment, courage, knowledge, reverence, and wonder and awe.

The Virtues

What are the virtues?

The virtues are spiritual powers or habits. The virtues help us to do what is good.

What are the most important virtues?

The most important virtues are the three virtues of faith, hope, and love. These virtues are gifts from God. They help us keep God at the center of our lives.

What is conscience?

Every person has a conscience. It is a gift God gives to every person. It helps us know and judge what is right and what is wrong. Our consciences move us to do good and avoid evil.

Evil and Sin

What is evil?

Evil is the harm we choose to do to one another and to God's creation.

What is temptation?

Temptations are feelings, people, and things that try to get us to turn away from God's love and not live a holy life.

What is sin?

Sin is freely choosing to do or say something that we know God does not want us to do or say.

What is mortal sin?

A mortal sin is doing or saying something on purpose that is very bad. A mortal sin is against what God wants us to do or say. When we commit a mortal sin, we lose sanctifying grace.

What are venial sins?

Venial sins are sins that are less serious than mortal sins. They weaken our love for God and for one another. They make us less holy.

Christian Prayer

What is prayer?

Prayer is talking to and listening to God. When we pray, we raise our minds and hearts to God the Father, Son, and Holy Spirit.

What is the Our Father?

The Lord's Prayer, or Our Father, is the prayer of all Christians. Jesus taught his disciples the Our Father. Jesus gave this prayer to the Church. When we pray the Our Father, we come closer to God and to his Son, Jesus Christ. The Our Father helps us become like Jesus.

What kinds of prayer are there?

Some kinds of prayer use words that we say aloud or quietly in our hearts. Some silent prayers use our imagination to bring us closer to God. Another silent prayer is simply being with God.

Glossary

angels
[page 68]

_____

- -

_____ are God's
messengers and helpers.

Baptism
[page 136]

_____

- -

_____ is the first
Sacrament that we celebrate. In Baptism, we receive
the gift of God's life and become members of the Church.

believe
[page 26]

_____

- -

To _____ means to have
faith in God.

Bible
[page 13]

_____

- -

The _____ is the written
Word of God.

Catholics
[page 106]

_____

- -

_____ are followers of
Jesus and members of the Catholic Church.

charity
[page 306]

_____

- -

_____ is loving others as
God loves us.

**children of
God**
[page 296]

_____

- -

All people are _____, created
in God's image.

Christians
[page 230]

_____

- -

_____ believe
in Jesus Christ and live as he taught.

Church
[page 102]

The _____ is the People of God who believe in Jesus and live as his followers.

Church year
[page 122]

The _____ is made up of four main seasons. They are Advent, Christmas, Lent, and Easter.

community
[page 266]

A _____ is a group of people who respect and care for one another.

counsel
[page 90]

_____ is another word for the help that a good teacher gives us. Counsel is a Gift of the Holy Spirit.

courage
[page 66]

The virtue of _____ helps us to trust in God and live our faith.

Creator
[page 35]

God is the _____. He created out of love and without any help.

cross
[page 80]

Jesus died on a _____ so that we could live forever in Heaven.

disciples
[page 149]

_____ are followers of Jesus.

Easter
[page 82]

_____ is the season when we celebrate that Jesus is risen.

Eucharist
[page 204]

The _____ is the Sacrament in which we receive the Body and Blood of Christ.

faith
[page 26]

_____ is a gift from God. It helps us to know God and to believe in him.

faithful
[page 12]

Good friends of Jesus are _____ to him. They are loyal to him.

fidelity
[page 156]

Parents demonstrate _____ when they love and care for their children.

Galilee
[page 212]

_____ was one of the main places where Jesus taught and helped people.

generosity
[page 24]

We share our things with others. We show _____ to them.

gentleness
[page 294]

Gentle people act calmly. They treat all people with _____ .

glory
[page 300]

_____ is another word for praise.

goodness
[page 144]

_____ is a sign that we are living our Baptism. When we are good to people, we honor God.

Gospel
[page 146]

The _____ is the Good News that Jesus told us about God's love.

Great Commandment
[page 270]

The _____ is to love God above all else and to love others as we love ourselves.

Holy Family
[page 52]

The _____ is the family of Jesus, Mary, and Joseph.

Holy Spirit
[page 92]

The _____ is the Third Person of the Holy Trinity.

Holy Trinity
[page 92]

The _____ is One God in Three Divine Persons—God the Father, God the Son, and God the Holy Spirit.

honor
[page 109]

We _____ people when we treat them with great respect.

hope
[page 78]

_____

The virtue of _____ helps us to remember that one day we may live in happiness with God forever in Heaven.

hospitality
[page 132]

_____

We demonstrate _____ when we welcome others as God's children.

humility
[page 318]

_____

_____ helps us know that all good things come from God.

image of God
[page 40]

_____

We are created in the _____.

joy
[page 202]

_____

We live with _____ when we recognize that true happiness comes from knowing and following Jesus.

justice
[page 264]

_____

We practice _____ when we treat people fairly.

kindness
[page 48]

_____

We live the virtue of _____ by treating others as we want to be treated.

Kingdom of God
[page 286]

_____

The _____ is Heaven. Heaven is happiness with God forever.

knowledge
[page 240]

The gift of _____ helps you to know and to follow God's rules.

marriage
[page 159]

A _____ is the lifelong promise of love made by a man and a woman to live as a family.

Mass
[page 197]

The _____ is the most important celebration of the Church.

Matrimony
[page 159]

_____ is the Sacrament that Catholics celebrate when they marry.

miracle
[page 216]

A _____ is something only God can do. It is a sign of God's love.

Our Father
[page 322]

The _____ is the prayer Jesus taught his disciples.

parable
[page 308]

Jesus often told a _____ to help people to know and love God better.

patience
[page 174]

We act with _____ when we listen carefully to others.

peace
[page 186]

_____

- -

We live as _____ makers
when we forgive those who have hurt us.

perseverance
[page 198]

_____

- -

_____ helps us to
live our faith when it is difficult.

prayer
[page 173]

_____

- - - - - - - - - - - - - - - - - -

_____ is listening and
talking to God.

prudence
[page 120]

_____

- - - - - - - - - - - - - - - - - -

_____ helps us ask
advice from others when making important decisions.

respect
[page 254]

_____

- -

We show people _____ when
we love them because they are children of God.

Resurrection
[page 83]

God's raising Jesus from the dead to new life is

_____

- -

called the _____ .

reverence
[page 102]

_____

- -

We show _____
to others when we honor them and give them great
respect.

Sacraments
[page 134]

_____

- -

The _____ are
the seven signs and celebrations of God's love that
Jesus gave the Church.

sin
[page 185]

_____

- - - - - - - - - - - - - - - - - -

_____ is choosing to do or say
something that we know is against God's laws.

Son of God
[page 50]

_____

- - - - - - - - - - - - - - - - - - - -

Jesus is the _____.

temperance
[page 252]

_____

- - - - - - - - - - - - - - - - - - - -

_____ helps
us to know the difference between what we need
and what we just want to have.

**Ten
Commandments**
[page 242]

_____

- - - - - - - - - - - - - - - - - - - -

The _____
are the ten laws that God has given us to help
us live as children of God.

understanding
[page 228]

God the Holy Spirit gives us the gift of
_____

- - - - - - - - - - - - - - - - - - - -

_____. Stories in
the Bible help us understand God's love for us.

wisdom
[page 210]

_____

- - - - - - - - - - - - - - - - - -

_____ helps us to know what
God wants us to do. It helps us to live a holy life.

wonder
[page 36]

_____

- - - - - - - - - - - - - - - - - - - -

_____ is a gift
from God to help us know how good he is.

worship
[page 165]

_____

- - - - - - - - - - - - - - - -

We _____ God when we love and
honor God more than anyone and anything else.

Index

Credits

Cover Illustration: Marcia Adams Ho

PHOTO CREDITS
Frontmatter: Page 6, © Laurence Monneret/Getty Images.
Chapter 1: Page 11, © Andersen Ross/Getty Images; 13, © Exactostock/SuperStock; 18, © KidStock/Blend Images/Getty Images; 18, © LWA/The Image Bank/ Getty Images; 21, © Ken Seet/Corbis; 22, © Ocean/ Corbis.
Chapter 2: Page 23, © Fever Images/Jupiterimages; 30, © Bill Wittman; 30, © Myrleen Pearson/PhotoEdit; 34, © Asia Images Group Pte Ltd/Alamy.
Chapter 3: Page 40, © Pressmaster/Shutterstock; 41, © Stockbroker/SuperStock; 41, © Jupiterimages/ Thinkstock; 46, © Comstock/Jupiterimages.
Chapter 4: Page 54, © Bounce/Getty Images; 54, © SW Productions/Design Pics Inc./Alamy; 54, © Fuse/Getty Images; 58, © Don Hammond/Design Pics Inc./Alamy; 59, © Collage Photography/Veer; 60, © Will Heap/ Getty Images.
Chapter 5: Page 65, © Roger Cracknell 01/classic/ Alamy; 69, © Jennie Woodcock; Reflections Photolibrary/CORBIS; 69, © Ruslan Dashinsky/ Getty Images; 70, © Tom Grill/Corbis; 70, © 2/Ocean/ Corbis; 71, © LWA/Jay Newman/Jupiterimages; 72, © liquidlibrary/Jupiterimages; 75, © Plush Studios/ Jupiterimages; 76, © Design Pics/Kristy-Anne Glubish/ Getty Images.
Chapter 6: Page 78, © VINCENZO PINTO/Staff/ AFP/Getty Images; 80, © iStockphoto/Thinkstock; 81, © Bill Wittman; 84, © Hemera/Thinkstock; 84, © Bill Wittman; 87, © Jose Luis Pelaez Inc/Jupiterimages; 88, © kali9/iStockphoto.
Chapter 7: Page 89, © iofoto/Shutterstock; 90, © Jane Tyson/iStockphoto; 90, © The Crosiers/Gene Plaisted, OSC; 92, © Michael O'Neil McGrath, OSFS BeeStillStudio.com 410.398.3057; 94, © Tischenko Irina/ Shutterstock; 95, © Fuse/Jupiterimages; 95, © Bruce Forster/Getty Images; 95, © Fuse/Jupiterimages; 96, © 28/Ocean/Corbis; 96, © 2/Ocean/Corbis; 99, © Bill Wittman; 100, © Jose Luis Pelaez Inc/Blend Images/Alamy.
Chapter 8: Page 103, © Bill Wittman; 103, © Thomas Tolstrup/Getty Images; 103, © Myrleen Pearson/ PhotoEdit; 103, © Bill Wittman; 106, © Stockbyte/ Thinkstock; 106, © Catholic News Service; 111, © Design Pics/Don Hammond/Jupiterimages; 112, © Ariel Skelley/Blend Images/Alamy; 113, © Steve Debenport/ Getty Images; 114, © JGI/Jamie Grill/Getty Images.
Chapter 9: Page 121, © iStockphoto/Thinkstock; 121, © iStockphoto/Thinkstock; 121, © BananaStock/ Thinkstock; 122, © Bill Wittman; 122, © Bill Wittman; 122, © Stephen McBrady/PhotoEdit; 122, © Bill Wittman; 126, © Darrel Tank/GoodSalt; 129, © Tetra Images/Jupiterimages; 130, © ADALBERTO ROQUE/ Staff/AFP/Getty Images.
Chapter 10: Page 134, © Dmitry Naumov/Shutterstock; 135, © Bill Wittman; 135, © Bill Wittman; 135, © JLP/Deimos/Corbis; 135, © Bill Wittman; 135, © Bill Wittman; 135, © Bill Wittman; 135, © Michael Newman/PhotoEdit; 136, © Bill Wittman; 137, © James Shaffer/PhotoEdit; 138, © Ted Foxx/Alamy; 141, © Alex Staroseltsev/Shutterstock; 142, © a la france/Alamy.
Chapter 11: Page 147, © De Agostini Picture Library/ The Bridgeman Art Library; 148, © Leland Bobbé/ Corbis; 150, © Bill Wittman; 153, © Bill Wittman; 154, © Michael Hitoshi/Jupiterimages.
Chapter 12: Page 155, © OJO Images/Jupiterimages; 156, © Jose Luis Pelaez Inc/Jupiterimages; 156, © Fancy/Veer/Corbis/Jupiterimages; 158, © Pacific Press/ GoodSalt; 159, © Comstock/Jupiterimages; 159, © Monkey Business Images/Shutterstock; 160, © Myrleen Pearson/PhotoEdit; 161, © Steve Hix/Somos Images/ Corbis; 165, © Fuse/Jupiterimages; 166, © Purestock/ Getty Images; 167, © Dave & Les Jacobs/Getty Images; 167, © AAGAMIA/Getty Images; 168, © Jose Luis Pelaez Inc/Getty Images.
Chapter 13: Page 173, © Tony Freeman/PhotoEdit; 176, © Brand X Pictures/Jupiterimages; 176, © Ruth Jenkinson/Dorling Kindersley/Getty Images; 177, © Bob Ingelhart/Getty Images; 179, © iStockphoto/Thinkstock; 179, © Illene MacDonald/PhotoEdit; 183, © The Crosiers/Gene Plaisted, OSC; 184, © Fuse/Jupiterimages.
Chapter 14: Page 186, © AFP/Stringer/AFP/Getty

Images; 188, © iStockphoto/Thinkstock; 190, © Image by Time Stops Photography/Flickr Open/Getty Images; 190, © Scholastic Studio 10/Photolibrary/Getty Images; 190, © BunnyHollywood/Getty Images; 192, © Steve Gorton/Getty Images; 195, © Myrleen Pearson/ PhotoEdit; 196, © moodboard/Alamy.
Chapter 15: Page 197, © SW Productions/Jupiterimages; 198, © Kristy-Anne Glubish/Design Pics Inc./Alamy; 199, © Siri Stafford/Thinkstock; 199, © George Doyle/ Thinkstock; 199, © JGI/Jamie Grill/Blend Images/Getty Images; 200, © Bill Wittman; 202, © Bill Wittman; 207, © Stockbyte/Jupiterimages; 208, © Bill Wittman.
Chapter 16: Page 209, © Juice Images/Jupiterimages; 210, © Jim Stipe/CRS; 210, © Jim Stipe/CRS; 212, © Peter Dennis/Getty Images; 216, © Ariel Skelley/Jupiterimages; 216, © SW Productions/Jupiterimages; 216, © Andersen Ross/Jupiterimages; 219, © iStockphoto/Thinkstock; 220, © Juice Images97/Juice Images/Alamy; 221, © iStockphoto/Thinkstock; 221, © iStockphoto/ Thinkstock; 222, © Mark Bowden/Getty Images.
Chapter 17: Page 227, © Alison Wright/Danita Delimont/Alamy; 230, © Comstock/Thinkstock; 230, © Todd Warnock/Thinkstock; 234, © Comstock Images/ Thinkstock; 234, © Myrleen Pearson/PhotoEdit; 237, © Inspirestock Inc./Alamy; 238, © Tony Freeman/PhotoEdit.
Chapter 18: Page 240, © 501room/Shutterstock; 240, © Ritu Manoj Jethani/Shutterstock; 240, © Neil Jacobs/ Getty Images; 243, © sonya etchison/Shutterstock; 244, © Colorblind/Jupiterimages; 244, © George Doyle/ Jupiterimages; 244, © Daniel Pangbourne/Jupiterimages; 246, © Bill Wittman; 246, © Christopher Futcher/E+/ Getty Images; 249, © Stockbyte/Jupiterimages; 250, © Goodshoot/Jupiterimages.
Chapter 19: Page 251, © Monkey Business Images/ Shutterstock; 252, © Tony Freeman/PhotoEdit; 253, © Martial Colomb/Photodisc/Getty Images; 253, © KidStock/Blend Images/Getty Images; 254, © Karl Kost/ Alamy; 254, © SW Productions/Getty Images; 258, © Jamie Grill/The Image Bank/Getty Images; 261, © Paul Burns/Jupiterimages; 262, © BananaStock/Jupiterimages.
Chapter 20: Page 263, © Zigy Kaluzny/Getty Images; 266, © Fuse/Jupiterimages; 266, © Tom Merton/ Jupiterimages; 266, © Colin Hawkins/Jupiterimages; 268, © Allen Donikowski/Flickr/Getty Images; 268, © Jose Luis Pelaez Inc/Blend Images/Getty Images; 273, © Brand X Pictures/Jupiterimages; 274, © 13/ Ocean/Corbis; 275, © Lon C. Diehl/PhotoEdit; 276, © Medioimages/Photodisc/Getty Images.
Chapter 21: Page 281, © Stockbyte/Getty Images; 282, © Photograph courtesy of the Pontifical Mission Societies; 283, © Michael Newman/PhotoEdit; 283, © Mary Kate Denny/ PhotoEdit; 283, © PhotoAlto/Laurence Mouton/Getty Images; 283, © Hill Street Studios/Eric Raptosh/Blend Images/Getty Images; 288, © Pressmaster/Shutterstock; 288, © GlowImage/Alamy; 288, © JR Carvey/Streetfly Studio/ Blend Images/Alamy; 291, © Digital Vision/Jupiterimages; 292, © Michael Newman/PhotoEdit.
Chapter 22: Page 294, © Bee Still Studio; 296, © iStockphoto/Thinkstock; 296, © Goodshoot/ Thinkstock; 296, © Photodisc/Thinkstock; 297, © Anthony Lee/OJO Images/Getty Images; 298, © Thomas M Perkins/Shutterstock; 300, © Leland Bobbe/ Jupiterimages; 303, © Zdorov Kirill Vladimirovich/ Shutterstock; 304, © Dave & Les Jacobs/Jupiterimages.
Chapter 23: Page 307, © Photononstop/SuperStock; 307, © Chris Clinton/Taxi/Getty Images; 307, © Comstock/Thinkstock; 312, © Fuse/Getty Images; 315, © Bill Wittman; 316, © Design Pics/SW Productions/ Jupiterimages.
Chapter 24: Page 317, © Bill Wittman; 318, © Jean-Claude FRANCOLON/Gamma-Rapho/Getty Images; 319, © Lisa Stirling/Digital Vision/Getty Images; 319, © Jupiterimages/Getty Images/Thinkstock; 322, © iStockphoto/Thinkstock; 322, © KidStock/Blend Images/ Getty Images; 324, © Peter Zander/Getty Images; 327, © Eric Audras/ONOKY - Photononstop/Alamy; 328, © Image Source/Jupiterimages; 329, © Tony Freeman/ PhotoEdit; 330, © Digital Vision./Getty Images.
Liturgical Seasons: Page 333, © Con Tanasiuk/ Design Pics Inc./Alamy; 334, © Chris Salvo/Getty Images; 334, © sodapix sodapix/Getty Images; 334, © ATTILA KISBENEDEK/Staff/AFP/Getty Images; 334, © The Crosiers/Gene Plaisted, OSC; 334, © H.

ARMSTRONG ROBERTS/ClassicStock/Alamy; 335, © John David Bigl III/Shutterstock; 337, © Stockbyte/ Jupiterimages; 337, © The Crosiers/Gene Plaisted, OSC; 337, © The Crosiers/Gene Plaisted, OSC; 337, © The Crosiers/Gene Plaisted, OSC; 337, © The Crosiers/Gene Plaisted, OSC; 339, © McPHOTO/SHU/ AgeFotostock; 341, © The Crosiers/Gene Plaisted, OSC; 341, © Amanda Brown/Star Ledger/Corbis; 343, © The Crosiers/Gene Plaisted, OSC; 345, © Baxter, Cathy (Contemporary Artist)/Bridgeman Art Library; 345, © Serp/Shutterstock; 346, © Spencer Grant/PhotoEdit; 349, © The Crosiers/Gene Plaisted, OSC; 351, © The Miami Herald, Walter Michot/AP Photo; 353, © Dejan Ristovski/Getty Images; 355, © Bill Wittman; 355, © The Crosiers/Gene Plaisted, OSC; 357, © Bill Wittman; 359, © The Crosiers/Gene Plaisted, OSC; 359, © Bill Wittman; 361, © Ocean/ Corbis; 361, © Bill Wittman; 361, © Cornelia Doerr/ Getty Images; 363, © The Crosiers/Gene Plaisted, OSC; 365, © The Crosiers/Gene Plaisted, OSC; 365, © Stephanie Neal Photography/Getty Images.
Backmatter: Page 367, ©Jupiterimages; 369, © Blend Images/Alamy; 372, © Bill Wittman; 373, © Bill Wittman; 374, © Bill Wittman; 375, © Bill Wittman; 376, © Bill Wittman; 377, © Bill Wittman; 379, © Bill Wittman; 380, © Universal Images Group Limited/Alamy; 380, © James Shaffer/PhotoEdit; 380 © Bill Wittman; 380, © Bob Mullen/The Catholic Photographer; 380, © Bob Mullen/The Catholic Photographer; 381, © Bill Wittman; 381, © Bob Mullen/The Catholic Photographer; 381, © Bill Wittman; 381, © Bill Wittman.

ILLUSTRATION CREDITS
Chapter 1: Page 9, Julia Woolf; 12, Q2A Media; 13–14, Robin Boyer; 16–17, Julia Woolf
Chapter 2: Page 24, Q2A Media; 25, Robin Boyer; 26, Julia Woolf; 28–29, Q2A Media; 33, Q2A Media
Chapter 3: Page 35, Q2A Media; 36, Kristin Sorra; 37, Linda Prater; 38, Burgandy Beam; 39, Q2A Media; 41, Robin Boyer; 43, Q2A Media
Chapter 4: Page 47, Julia Woolf; 48, Q2A Media; 49, George Hamblin; 50–51, Julia Woolf; 52, Q2A Media; 53, Julia Woolf; 57, Q2A Media.
Chapter 5: Page 63, Julia Woolf; 66, Q2A Media; 67, Jamie Pogue; 68, Julia Woolf.
Chapter 6: Page 77, Julia Woolf; 82, Julia Woolf; 83, Jamie Pogue
Chapter 7: Page 91, Q2A Media
Chapter 8: Page 101, Q2A Media; 102, Q2A Media; 104, Julia Woolf; 108, Q2A Media.
Chapter 9: Page 117, Julia Woolf; 120, Q2A Media; 123, Q2A Media; 124, Q2A Media; 125, Jamie Pogue
Chapter 10: Page 131, Julia Woolf; 132, Q2A Media; 133, Remy Simard
Chapter 11: Page 143, Julia Woolf; 144, Q2A Media; 145, Jamie Pogue; 146, Kristin Sorra; 149, Q2A Media; 151, Q2A Media; 152, Q2A Media
Chapter 12: Page 157, Jamie Pogue; 160, Q2A Media; 162, Julia Woolf
Chapter 13: Page 171, Julia Woolf; 174–175, Q2A Media; 178, Q2A Media; 123, Q2A Media.
Chapter 14: Page 185, Sole Otero; 189, Q2A Media; 191, Q2A Media; 193, Q2A Media
Chapter 15: Page 201, Q2A Media; 204, Julia Woolf.
Chapter 16: Page 211, Jamie Pogue; 213, Lyn Boyer; 214, Julia Woolf; 215, Ivanovs
Chapter 17: Page 225, Julia Woolf; 228, Q2A Media; 232–233, Julia Woolf
Chapter 18: Page 239, Ivanke and Lola; 242, Jamie Pogue
Chapter 19: Page 255, Rémy Simard; 256, Q2A Media; 257, Rémy Simard.
Chapter 20: Page 264, Colleen Madden; 265, Jamie Pogue; 267, Jamie Pogue; 269, Q2A Media; 270, Q2A Media.
Chapter 21: Page 279, Julia Woolf; 284–285, Kristin Sorra; 286–287, Julia Woolf
Chapter 22: Page 293, Julia Woolf; 295, Q2A Media; 296, Jamie Pogue; 299, Rémy Simard
Chapter 23: Page 305, Julia Woolf; 306, Q2A Media; 308–309, Q2A Media; 310, Julia Woolf; 311, Rémy Simard
Chapter 24: Page 320, Ivanovs
Liturgical Seasons: Page 344, Pamela Becker; 354, Ivanke and Lola; 366, Ivanke and Lola